D0498377

A General Theory of

AUTHORITY

A General Theory of

AUTHORITY

by

YVES R. SIMON

With an Introduction by

A. ROBERT CAPONIGRI

UNIVERSITY OF NOTRE DAME PRESS · 1962

INTRODUCTION

IN THE PRESENT WORK THE LATE PROFESSOR YVES SIMON RETURNS
to the theme which was central to his philosophical interest almost from the beginning of his academic career: *authority*. His
earliest treatment of this theme in English was the Aquinas Lecture at Marquette University for the year 1940: *The Nature
and Functions of Authority*. In the preface of this brief work,
which, within certain restricted circles, has already achieved
something of the stature of a classic, Professor Simon states that
he is reporting on the current status of an inquiry which he had
begun many years before. The reference seems to be—at least
in part—to the earlier French work, *Critique de la Connais-
sance Morale* (1934); in this work he had devoted extensive consideration to the ontology and the epistemology of the prudential judgment, an issue very central to his whole consideration
of authority.

The formulation of his thought on authority in the Aquinas
Lecture achieved a clarity of order and a conciseness which was
not to be surpassed in any later writing on the matter. Despite
this fact, it is to his work, *The Philosophy of Democratic Government* (1951), that one must turn for the exposition of his
theory in its mature form. When it was proposed to include in
the anthology, *Modern Catholic Thinkers* (1960), a selection
dealing with authority from this last-named work, Professor
Simon agreed, provided that he might subject the passage to
further revision and refinement. Although possessing considerable interest in itself, this revision left his thought on the matter basically intact. It was contrary to Professor Simon's nature
ever to feel that he had dealt adequately with any problem. His
insight into philosophical problems was both authentic and
profound, and he saw, almost with an artist's eye, the discrepancy between any achieved position and the problem to which

it related. At the same time, the "demon of perfection," as Paul
Elmer More once called it, drove him hard. It was inevitable,
therefore, that he should return to the problem, as he does in
these present pages. By speaking of a "general theory" of authority, Professor Simon makes it clear that he sought to transcend
those circumstantial limits which had defined his earlier treat-
ments. The effort is genuine and there can be no doubt but that
his view on the nature of authority and its functions has, in
these pages, resulted in a new dimension, enriching to a very
considerable extent the fundamental statement he had already
achieved. It is a most fitting conclusion to a lifetime of labor
and concern.

To speak only circumstantially about his treatment of the
problem of authority would, however, fail to do justice to Professor Simon. For he was above all a substantive philosopher,
concerned with real, and not merely formal problems, and seek-
ing substantive and committed positions. It is what he has to
say about the matter that counts and this, he would insist, must
be placed in the forefront of any consideration. We may therefore devote a few paragraphs to a consideration of his theory of
authority in its substantive aspect .

To seek out the basic sources of Professor Simon's concern
with the problem of authority—as the clue to his treatment and
doctrine—is indeed an irresistible temptation. The answer
which emerges from this inquiry is as arresting as it is illuminating: he is fascinated by authority precisely because he is so intensely devoted to freedom, to liberty. This statement invites
reflection, not simply because of the paradox it seemingly contains, but because it genuinely illuminates the sources of
Simon's thought, and prepares one for the concrete position he
later develops and the line of argument he employs to attain it.

Simon's passionate attachment to liberty was naturally come
by. It was integral to his cultural inheritance as a Frenchman,
for whom the great revolution of 1789 remained one of the central events of modern history. Liberty, equality, fraternity—the
great shibboleths of that revolution—always remained, for Simon, objects of the most intense affirmation. His attachment to
them was deepened, rather than lessened, by the fact that he

could not accept the theoretical bases on which they had been affirmed in the revolutionary context. Those bases had been laicist, secularist, rationalist, in the pejorative sense of the term. These he sought to replace by bases drawn from the religious tradition of Christianity—without yielding one iota of the terminative concepts of liberty, equality and fraternity.

At the same time, his attachment to these values encountered —not merely at the level of intellectual reflection, but in the depth of his spirit—an immovable obstacle and counterpoise: his profound insight into the primacy of order. Indeed, if one were to ask which of these attachments marked his spirit more characteristically, it would be necessary to reply: order. His sense for and evaluation of order had about it a certain elemental quality. One sensed that it was rooted in the order of the seasons, in the earth beneath his feet, even while it ascended through the grades of being to the celestial realms, the range of human society, and ultimately, the divine ordinance of all things. Elemental and revolutionary, Jacobin and Norman son of the earth and sky—these things Simon then was, and forever remained; order and liberty provide the poles between which the tensions of his spirit were drawn taut.

These attachments are illuminating because they lead us at once to both the heart of his concern for authority and to the heart of his doctrine about it. The organic need of his mind and spirit was for a principle of unity between the ostensibly diverse demands of freedom and order. Authority attracted him because he saw in it the principle of synthesis he sought: an order which generated and guaranteed liberty, a liberty which found its highest expression in order. This is what authority was and remained for him: the ground of this synthesis, the demiurge of the only world his spirit could inhabit with ease.

Simon's concrete analysis of authority bears out this insight in sustained detail. He never doubted that to create this synthesis was the supreme duty and essence of authority. So firm and unshaken was he in this certainty that he tends, mainly, to be concerned with the mechanics of authority, or its *functions* as he prefers to call them. It is essential to insist, however, that these functions are *not,* for him, incidental or transitive characteristics of authority. Rather, they constitute its very essence. They constitute the dialectical movement through which authority achieves the synthesis of order guaranteeing freedom, of freedom expressing itself as order. Once one has grasped his central insight, the detailed development of his thought follows with a certain sense of inevitability.

This characteristic of Simon's thought brings him eventually to the confrontation of authority and law. The ground of this confrontation is clear. The power of synthesis between order and freedom which he ascribes to authority, modern thought has tended to assign rather to law; even more, modern thought has tended to see in law, as Simon sees in authority, not the mere instrument, but the actuality of this synthesis. Simon engages this issue directly and without evasion. The precedence which he assigns to authority rests upon what might be called the pragmatic or even existential element in his thought. The measure of all, in this issue, is social effectiveness; he is looking for the principle of effective synthesis. Since he insists that the field of this effectiveness is action—the unified action of a multitude of persons—the principle cannot be of any other character. It too must exhibit the property of the person. The synthesis of law appears to him to be too abstract, too remote from the order and realm of action, to provide an effective principle of synthesis.

An opponent might find it quite easy to point out a flaw in his position: the concept of law with which he operated. Simon's model for the notion of law is drawn from the natural sciences. By contrast, one whose basic insight into law is sociological must possess a far more concrete and effective notion of it. The sociological viewpoint achieves a concreteness which not only endows law with that effectiveness which Simon made the measure of all else in the issue, but also renders it immune from that element of indetermination which must always attach itself to the notion of the person.

Simon's indelible suspicion of pure legalism is contagious. It does not necessarily lead, however, in the direction he takes. Rather, it can be made the basis for an additional discernment: that in the alleged antithesis between authority and law, one is confronted by an inconclusive alternative. Simon implies that a decision must be made on a monistic basis: authority, involving personal agency and decision, or law. Such monism, however, can become a source of confusion in social analysis. In its place a pluralism of principles recommends itself as more adequate to some critics.

In any event, Simon's entire address to authority in the present work, as in the earlier works which it continues and fulfills, is a source of the most enlightening reflection. The qualities of his thought are those which must inevitably recommend it to all serious inquirers: a controlled urgency of problem, a firm and sure touch in analysis, an engaging caution in synthesis and conclusion, and throughout, a shining humility and sincerity which unfailingly places issues above opinions, conviction above persuasion, logic above rhetoric.

A. ROBERT CAPONIGRI
University of Notre Dame

CONTENTS

    It seems most fitting to dedicate this book to the two institutions in America which afforded my husband the great opportunity of teaching and research in an atmosphere of intense intellectual stimulation and friendship: The University of Notre Dame and the Committee on Social Thought at the University of Chicago. The present work is to a large degree the result of the opportunities provided by these universities.

—MRS. YVES R. SIMON

October 1962

CHAPTER 1

The Bad Name of Authority

The issue of authority has such a bad reputation that a philosopher cannot discuss it without exposing himself to suspicion and malice. Yet authority is present in all phases of social life. The skill of anarchist thinkers may lend verisimilitude to systems marked by extensive dependence upon good will, tolerance, mutual understanding, persuasion and consent. But, within these pictures of smoothly operating institutions, authority is unmistakably present, or, if it is not, verisimilitude disappears and what is left is a lifeless mimicry of social relations. Why is it that men distrust so intensely a thing without which they cannot, by all evidences, live and act together?

As a matter of common experience, subjection to authority causes much discomfort and mortification; it involves the permanent foundation of an ever threatening, if not ever present, distress. But reluctance to bear such distress does not sufficiently account for the bad name of authority. Over and above this obvious reluctance, aversion to authority derives energy from sublime sources. Its really formidable power originates in the loftiest inclinations of the human soul. The case would be relatively simple and easy to deal with if the enemies of authority were only pride and passion. The fact is that authority is reputed to conflict with justice, life, truth and order.

AUTHORITY IN SEEMING CONFLICT WITH JUSTICE

The common way to secure a good or service is to surrender a good or service held equal in value. In a society where such method generally obtains, the services of plumbers and carpenters, as well as those of physicians and lawyers, are purchased at unpleasantly high cost. No wonder that some people feel a nostalgia for circumstances where an upper position gives a right to an abundance of facilities. Prices and wages forcibly kept low do not balance the goods and services procured. The exchange is unequal; more exactly, the transaction has only in part the character of an exchange; part of the service rendered is a tribute describable as the privilege of authority and disquietingly reminiscent of the stated sums which used to be paid periodically to the pirates of Barbary. The notion of authority thus comes to be associated with that of an exchange disrupted by sheer might.

AUTHORITY IN SEEMING CONFLICT WITH LIFE

Actions ordered by authority originate outside the agent; they bear a mark of externality in contrast with the spontaneousness which characterizes the operations of nature and life.[1] Suppose that the things procured are

1 "That alone was right which was done of one's own inner conviction and mere motion, that was lifeless and evil which was done out of obedience to any external authority." F. Pollock, Introduction to William K. Clifford's *Lectures and Essays* (London: Macmillan, 1901), vol. I, 44.

altogether good: the fact that they are procured by authority still denies them the cherished perfection of proceeding from within. A man can behave well either because he is told to do so or by his own inclination. Good behavior obtained by commandment and obedience is still held defective inasmuch as it lacks spontaneity, life, voluntariness, liberty. The ideal subject of authoritarian rule would display all the submissiveness and determinateness of a machine. Other things being equal, a state of affairs brought about vitally is preferable to a state of affairs brought about mechanically. It may even be argued that lesser results obtained through vital processes are more valuable than greater results obtained by curbing the forces of life. Authority boasts of unique ability to assure peace: but the peace it procures is that of death.—*They make a solitude, and call it peace* (Tacitus). Even when the effects intended are in line with nature, the way in which authority brings them about involves a sort of violence.

Authority becomes more detestable as the things subjected to its methods increase in dignity and pertain more directly to what is vital and spiritual in man. If, in order to cut down the rate of accidents, it is held expedient that street traffic be governed in machine-like fashion by the agents of an irresistible power, so let it be. The sacrifice of some spontaneity at the wheel of a car is not a very serious one. But when a power pretends to shape the moral personality of citizens, their beliefs, their tastes and their loves, the time for anger has come. Authority, if needed at all, should be relegated to the domains where lifelessness is least destructive. If, through the mechanization of less important functions, it helps to liberate the higher forms of life, so much the better. But keep it away from things noble and spiritual, and do not attempt to force a soul into this enemy of life.

AUTHORITY IN SEEMING CONFLICT WITH TRUTH

Among the lofty things that authority is reputed to threaten is the respect of our minds for truth. The anger commonly aroused by the notion that authority might supersede the power of truth is a metaphysical sentiment of great significance. We all have some experience of situations in which a problem of truth happens to be unjustifiably answered by submission to authority. Thus, if often happens that in international disputes incompatible versions of the same event are held by diverse governments; to spare ourselves the pangs of anxiety, the labors of research, and sometimes the humiliation of having been wrong, we may make it a rule that our assent will go to the version officially held by the government which is ours. A similar situation is common in the conflict of political parties and in dialogues between schools of thought. Our daily life is constantly troubled by vexing questions, ideological, ethical, political, esthetic, and factual, to which we cannot remain indifferent, to which we must give some sort of answer, and which involve such obscurities that an answer in terms of objective determination is very hard to reach. But most of the time these questions admit of cheap, easy, pacifying, and heartening answers if we make it a set rule to repeat what authority has said. The lovers of truth easily come to suspect that the whole system of authority is a pragmatic device, designed to spare weak souls the hardship of finding truth and abiding by it.

No doubt, grounds for suspecting an antagonistic relation between authority and truth are as old as human reason and human testimony. However, such suspicion assumed a more determinate form and a greater power when, some time in the eighteenth century, the ideal of a social science built after the pattern of physics got hold of minds and imaginations. The essentials of this epoch-making adventure can be summed up as follows: Western men had become aware that their control over physical nature was immensely increased whenever scientific propositions replaced common experience as the theoretical basis of their action. As far as physical nature is concerned, wonders can be worked by arts grounded in scientific formulas. Why should it be impossible to do for society what is being done so successfully in the realm of physical nature? Why should it be impossible to work out a social science patterned after physics, and like physics objective, impersonal, free from anthropomorphic bias, free from value judgments, exact, rigorous, indifferent to national or personal whims and preferences, necessary, and irresistible? From such a science a rational art would be derived, and the proper conduct of societies would be insured by the impersonal decisions of enlightened reason. In the construct of a society ruled by the power of social science, authority plays no part. This construct helps us to understand why authority plays such an overwhelming part in societies ignorant of social science. We are wondering about the proper way to attain a certain goal and, because of our inability to demonstrate scientifically which way is the proper one, we would deliberate indefinitely did we not agree to follow the decisions of authority. These may not be the

best possible ones, but they are still   preferable to indefinitely protracted irresolution. The case is like that
of Descartes' travelers, lost in the midst of a forest.[2] By
moving constantly in the same direction, they will reach
a place which may not be the best but where they will
certainly be better off than in the midst of a forest. Not
knowing which way to take, but realizing that movement in any clear direction is better than unending idle-
ness, we let authority decide which way we shall take,
and we admire its ability to substitute definite action for
endless deliberation. In the enthusiastic visions of early
social science, such a state of affairs constitutes, according to an expression used by Karl Marx in a different
connection, the prehistory of society. Genuinely human
history begins when the travelers in the forest are provided by science with rational, objective, definite, and
demonstrated methods of knowing which way to take in
order to reach the place where they want to go. For the
most audacious, social science would not only solve the
conditional problem of selecting the way on the basis of
an established intention of the goal; it would resolve,
just as well, the problem of the goal to be intended.
Authority would no longer have anything to do either
with regard to the means or with regard to the end. It
has a role to play as long as common action, by reason of
ignorance, remains subject to looseness, flexibility, uncertainty. But as soon as mature reason, i.e., reason per-
fected by science, proposes definite forms of action according to truth, the method of authority becomes sheer
deception. Of this method of deception, what can be the
purpose if not just the advantage of the men or classes
in power?

[2] *Discourse on Method,* Third Part.

AUTHORITY IN SEEMING CONFLICT WITH ORDER

The principle of authority has often been challenged by the spirit of disorder. It is a common belief that order inevitably implies suppressions, restrictions, curtailments, and violent destruction; hence the notion that any excess of order impairs life and that unorganized spontaneity must be defended and promoted for the sake of life itself. The conflict between life and authority, outlined in the foregoing, often appears as a particular case of a deeper conflict between life and order. Romanticism is famous for its rebels, enamoured of the most ebullient phases of life, and inebriated with the spring-like character of vital activity. Clearly, insofar as an opposition can be construed between understanding and nature, the phases of life to which the romantic revolt is dedicated belong to the realm of nature rather than to that of understanding. Life, as exalted by the romantic revolt, resembles prime matter in the description of St. Augustine:[3] in a first approximation, it seems to be a tempestuous stream of weird forms; but, as intuition grows in intensity, the forms disappear and no longer hinder the glory of a thing which is mobility, storm and drive, creativeness and unpredictability. In such a system of passionate intuitions, disorder, whether this name is used or not, assumes an appearance akin to that of life itself. The romantic rebel fights authority precisely because he sees in it a factor of order.

Yet it also happens that a spirit of dedication to order brings about a particular form of opposition to authority. The rules which create order in mankind are either laws or contractual arrangements. Authority may con-

[3] *Confessions,* Bk. XII, 6.6.

flict with both. Indeed, laws are counted among the works of authority. But it should also be remarked that the more a law is universal, natural and impersonal, the more it has the character of a law, whereas the distinctive features of authority are more intensely present in the particular and the contingent law than in the universal and necessary one, in the decree than in the law, in the decree regulating matters strictly determined with regard to here and now than in the decree concerned with somewhat general cases, and in the command marked by the personality of a leader than in an anonymous and impersonal ordinance. Briefly: whereas the law is attracted by an ideal of rational impersonality, acts of authority tend toward a state of concreteness involving the personalities of men, and all the contingencies to which human wills are subject. Considered in its contrast with law, authority seems to be connected with human arbitrariness, by all means the worst enemy of order. As to the contractual settlement, it is essentially a rule of exchange, consequently an equalitarian rule. Order obtains in exchange relations when, regardless of all the ways in which the exchanging parties may be unequal, a free discussion has procured a sound approximation to definite equality between the exchanged values. When there is no problem except that of determining what value is equal to what value, any act of authority is a disruption of order.

HYPOTHESIS: AUTHORITY EMBRACES A COMPLEX OF FUNCTIONS

Arguments derived from justice, life, truth, and order constitute a powerful prejudice against authority. In spite of this, anarchy is rarely or never upheld with qualified consistency. In the pedagogy of Rousseau, there is a set purpose to let the child be guided by natural necessity rather than by human command, and to let him learn from the experience of physical facts rather than by obedience. "Keep the child solely dependent on things; you will have followed the order of Nature in the process of his upbringing. Never oppose to his unreasonable wishes any but physical obstacles or punishments resulting from the actions themselves—he will remember these punishments in similar situations. It is enough to prevent him from doing evil without forbidding him to do it. . . ."[4] Remarkably, the theory that the method of authority is a poor substitute for the pedagogical power of nature has been accepted, in varying degree of enthusiasm or reluctance, by all schools of pedagogy and has demonstrated lasting power. Yet the authority of parents and tutors is present throughout pedagogical theories, even when it is passed over in silence. Childhood is the domain where the suppression of all authority is obviously impossible. The most radical constructs of anarchy, as soon as they rise above the level of idle rhetoric, must admit of qualifications so far as the immature part of mankind is concerned. Anti-authoritarian theorists, with few exceptions if any, do not mean that authority should disappear or that it can ever cease to be a factor of major importance in human affairs. What the thinkers opposed to authority generally mean is that authority can never be vindicated except by such deficiencies as are found in children, in the feeble-minded, the emotionally unstable, the criminally inclined, the illiterate, and the historically primitive. The real problem is not whether authority must wither away: no doubt, it will always play an all-

[4] *Emile,* II. Amsterdam, Jean Neaulme, 1762.

important part in human affairs. *The problem is whether deficiencies alone cause authority to be necessary.* It is obvious, indeed, that in many cases the need for authority originates in some defect and disappears when sufficiency is attained. But the commonly associated negation, viz., that authority never originates in the positive qualities of man and society, is by no means obvious and should not be received uncritically. The supposition that authority, in certain cases and domains, is made necessary not by deficiencies but by nature—this supposition is not evidently absurd. To hold, in some aprioristic way, that it does not deserve examination would merely evince wishful thinking of the least scientific kind. The truth may well be that authority has several functions, some of which would be relative to deficient states of affairs and others to features of perfection.

Throughout the following studies, we propose to try the theory that authority must be analyzed into a plurality of functions. But attitudes ignore analyses and commonly lump together heterogeneous aspects never considered in their distinct intelligibility. An analytical study of functions is perhaps all that is needed to ascertain the relation of authority to justice, to life, to truth, and to order. If the relation between authority and these cherished values was successfully clarified, unexpected reconciliations would take place, and improved circumstances would be provided for the dialogue of the philosophers on the fundamental problems of society.

CHAPTER 2

Common Good
and Common Action

If any functions of authority originate in nature and plenitude rather than in deficiency, it can be reasonably conjectured that they are relative to common existence and common action. Granted that in many cases authority merely substitutes for self-government, the theory that it also has essential functions must be tested first in the field of community life. But the definition of this field presupposes an inquiry, no matter how brief, into human sociability.

GROUNDS AND FORMS OF SOCIABILITY

THE NEEDS OF THE INDIVIDUAL

It is perfectly obvious that the needs of the individual call for the association of men; yet significant implications of this proposition are commonly ignored. For one thing, the notion of individual need is often restricted, in most arbitrary fashion, to needs of a biological, physical, material character. The necessity of mutual assistance and division of labor in the fight against hunger and thirst, cold, wild beasts, and disease is more commonly

23

expressed than the immense and almost constantly increased service that society renders to individuals in intellectual, esthetic, moral, and spiritual life. Any improper emphasis on the physical needs served by society suggests that the purposes and the requirements of social life are contained within a sphere of material goods. Concomitantly, it is often taken for granted that the goods of the spirit are altogether individual and that their pursuit is an entirely individualistic concern. Thus, human life would be split into a part socialized by material needs and a nobler part distinguished both by spirituality and individual independence. To dispose of this construct, just think of what a beginner in the sciences owes to the daily assistance of society. A comparison between a student in our universities and a man self-educated in the wilderness would involve a good deal of fiction, but we have all the data needed to compare, with regard to proficiency, students separated by a few generations. In the fields where the social life of the understanding is most successful—mathematics, physics . . .— the men of the younger generation can solve, with the resources of ordinary intelligence, problems which were hardly treatable for geniuses of earlier ages.

By another unwarranted restriction of meaning, it is often held that a need is necessarily self-centered. In fact, the notion of need expresses merely the state of a tendency not yet satisfied with ultimate accomplishment. Among the tendencies which make up the dynamism of a rational being, some are self-centered and some are generous; all admit of a state of need, and the need to give is no less real than the need to take. Consider the grounds of friendship and the ways in which a man is related to his friends. A young fellow, uncertain about what he is and what he wants to be, with little background, no estate, no steady position, with much anxiety, will be looking for friends in a context of self-centered needs. No ethically unfavorable connotation attaches to the notion of a need centered about the self. Whether the center of a need is within the self or beyond it depends upon the nature of the tendency involved and is antecedent to moral use. Needs relative to such goods as food and shelter are self-centered by nature and remain self-centered in the most disinterested man despite all the generosity which enters into his way of satisfying his needs and of relating their satisfaction to further ends.

But some needs have their center beyond the self; a man whose personality features contrast with those of the young fellow described just above still needs friends. He does not depend on the help of friends for food or shelter, for his fortune is already made; he is not in the least motivated by the expectation of physical care in case of disease, for he is in good health and anyway has little fear of disease and death; neither does it occur to him that he may need friendly attention to soothe him in case of emotional disaster, for his nervous balance is well assured; and he does not feel that the company of friends is necessary to him as protection against boredom, for he does so well in the company of his ideas, his memories, his books and familiar belongings that the threat of boredom is not felt. We are describing a distinguished instance of mature development, strength of character, soundness, dominating indifference, freedom. Yet this accomplished person needs the company of beloved ones, inasmuch as his very state of accomplishment intensifies in him every generous trait and every tendency to act by way of superabundance. He needs to give. True, the center of the act of giving is found in the beneficiary of the gift, and the gift is primarily designed to satisfy a need in the receiver. Yet the gift satisfies also a need in the giver. Such a non-self-centered need may attain a high degree of intensity. The accomplished person whom we are considering would be unhappy if he knew no children to please with Christmas presents, and his home-coming from happy journeys would be gloomy if no one expected him to bring jewelry or dresses from the remote land. His knowledge would give him little joy if he had no chance to impart it to eager intellects, and the very firmness of his character would seem to him a tedious advantage if it should never result in a friend's achieving greater mastery over himself.

For the sake of clarity, we have used the example of a firm and accomplished person to describe other-centered needs. In such persons generosity is most obviously noticeable. However, other-centered needs exist in all; they secretly move the last of men. To appreciate the power and the social significance of other-centered needs in everyone, it suffices to remark that in case of frustration the tendency to act generously becomes the most redoubtable of antisocial drives. Men would rather stand physical destitution than be denied opportunity for disinterested love and sacrifice.

The Common Good

The question now arises whether the needs of the individual are the only cause of human association and whether, correspondingly, society has no purpose beyond the satisfaction of individual needs. The word "individualism," which so often is made worthless by confusion, admits of a precise sense insofar as it designates

the theory that the single purpose of society is the service
of the individual. The individualistic interpretation of
sociability appeals to souls trained in humane disciplines
and possessed of an exacting sense for the human character of everything that pertains to society. As soon as it
is suggested that the purpose of human effort lies in an
achievement placed beyond the individual's good, a
suspicion arises that human substance may be ultimately
dedicated to things as external to man as the pyramids of
Egypt. In all periods of history, voluminous facts signify
that under the name of common good, republic, father-
land, empire, what is actually pursued may not be a good
state of human affairs but a work of art designed to provide its creator with the inebriating experience of creation. The joy of the creator assumes unique intensity
when the thing out of which the work of art is made is
human flesh and soul. The artist's rapture is greatest
when he uses as matter of his own creation not marble
and brass but beings made after the image of God. "The
finest clay, the most precious marble—man—is here
kneaded and hewn. . . ."[1] True, the common good conceived as a work of art and a thing external to man is
merely a corruption of the genuine common good. In
this world of contingency, every form or process admits
of imitation; in human affairs, counterfeit is often so
related to the genuine form that it appears, with disquieting frequency, precisely where the genuine form is
most earnestly sought. An inquiry into the common good
must involve constant awareness that its object may, at
any time, be displaced by deadly counterfeit.

To answer the question of whether the association of

[1] F. Nietzsche, *The Birth of Tragedy* (Garden City, N.Y.:
Doubleday Anchor Books, 1956), p. 24.

men is designed to serve not only the needs of the individual but also goods situated beyond individual achievement, we should turn our attention, first, to the limitations of individual plenitude; then we may be able to understand, just by glancing at the daily life of human communities, how these limitations are transcended.

Individuals are narrowly restricted with regard to diversity, and inevitable circumstances hold in check the desire for totality which belongs to rational nature. In terms of essential causality, there is no reason why one and the same man should not be painter, musician, philosopher, captain of industry, and statesman. In fact, personalities developed excellently on more than a very few lines are extremely rare, and significant limitations can easily be found in Leonardo da Vinci and Goethe. The rule to which all men are subjected in varying degree is one of specialization for the sake of proficiency. This rule entails heavy sacrifices even in the most gifted. A man highly successful in his calling accomplishes little in comparison with the ample virtualities of man. He has failed in a hundred respects. Only the union of many can remedy the failure of each. But of all the restrictions inflicted upon the boundless ambition of our rational nature, the most painful concerns the duration of individual achievements. Within the temporal order we would feel hopeless if the virtual immortal life of the community did not compensate for the brevity of individual existence. Death is known to be particularly hard and surrounded with anxiety for those who end their days in individualistic loneliness.

These are the familiar facts referred to by a well known text of Aristotle, ordinarily summed up in the following words, "The common good is greater and more divine than the private good."[2] "Greater" expresses a higher degree of perfection with regard both to duration and to diversity. "Divine," as translating the Greek *theion*, does not designate so much a godlike essence as a participation in the privilege of imperishability. In this world of change, individuals come and go. The law of generation and corruption covers the whole universe of nature. This law is transcended in a very proper sense by the incorruptibility of the species and the immortality of human association. The masterpiece of the natural world cannot be found in the transient individual. Nor can it be found in the species, which is not imperishable except in the state of universality; but in this state it is no longer unqualifiedly real. Human communities are the highest attainments of nature, for they are virtually unlimited with regard to diversity of perfections, and virtually immortal. Beyond the satisfaction of individual needs the association of men serves a good unique in plenitude and duration, the common good of the human community.

PARTNERSHIP AND COMMUNITY

Before we are ready to state the problem of authority, we still need to inquire into the basic forms of association. These are the mere partnership and the community. Let us consider familiar examples. A merchant succeeds in convincing an owner of capital that money invested in his business would bring nice dividends. By the terms of their contract, any profits will be divided according to a definite ratio. Then the merchant goes to the market, and the money-lender sits back and awaits the event. Their "common interest" was celebrated in ex-

[2] *Eth.* 1.2. 1094b7.

pectant toasts, but they are not engaged in any common action designed to promote any "common interest." The merchant works by himself or with his employees; he does not work with the money-lender, who remains a silent partner. Where there is no common action, there is no common good. These two men do not make up a community. What they call their "common interest" is in fact a sum of private interests that happen[3] to be interdependent.

In contradistinction to mere partners, the members of a community—family, factory, football team, army, state, church . . .—are engaged in a common action whose object is qualitatively different from a sum of interdependent goods. Whereas the contractual relation is normally the sufficient rule of the mere partnership, our problem is precisely to decide whether the community normally calls for the kind of rule known as authority.

To conclude this preliminary inquiry, let us remark that contract and community can be related in diverse ways. (1) The association established by contract may be of such nature that the relation between the associates remains exclusively contractual. The money-lender and the merchant exemplify such a case. (2) The association founded by contract may be of such nature as to involve a common action. When they sign a contract, partners

[3] The notion of contingency conveyed by "happen" is understood here with strict propriety. The fact that the capital of the enterprise, or part of it, is owned by a lender, is accidental to the commercial operations: these would not be essentially different if the merchant had inherited all the capital he needs. Consider, on the other hand, the cooperation of the surgeon, his assistant, the anesthetist and the nurses in the treatment of a surgical case: it would not occur to anybody to say that the purposes of these persons just "happen" to be interdependent. Their unity is not a sheer happening.

may be entering into a society which is not a mere partnership. Such is the case, for instance, in the hiring of labor. Production demands that manager and laborer act together, and neither has the character of a silent partner. However, communities of this type can, in most instances, be dissolved at will, or according to terms specified by the initial contract. (3) The community founded by contract may not be dissoluble at will. It may even be of such nature as not to be dissoluble at all. Because the contract is the only rule of the mere partnership, it is commonly assumed, by unwarranted inference, that persons associated by contract necessarily remain mere partners and can dissolve their association. The relation between man and wife involves a character of stability determined by the very nature of the man-and-wife community. Yet this community was founded by contract.

If nothing abnormal occurs, the need for authority is never felt in a relation of mere partnership. The contractual arrangement which, as such, is absolutely equalitarian, suffices. A decision by authority will be necessary only if the working of the contract is impeded by such accidents as misunderstanding, bad faith, or unforeseen conjuncture. Thus, if all human societies were mere partnerships, authority would never be needed except on account of some fault or accident. The deficiency theory of authority would be entirely vindicated.

THE UNITY OF COMMON ACTION

Assuming now the features proper to the kind of association described as a community, let us state the problem of united action. Every community is relative to a good to be sought and enjoyed in common. But, by the very fact that a community comprises a number of individuals, the unity of its action cannot be taken for granted: it has to be caused. Further, if the community is to endure, the cause of its united action must be firm and stable. Since rational agents are guided by judgment, the problem of bringing about unity in the action of men resolves into the problem of insuring the unity of their practical judgment. For example, the family community would cease to exist if each member did not judge—for one reason or another—that he ought to reside in this particular locality and in this particular house. A farm would soon be ruined if those engaged in the production of wheat did not all judge—again, for one reason or another—that these fields ought to be put into wheat this year. A factory could not operate if the members of its personnel did not all judge that a definite schedule ought to be observed. A deliberating assembly is indeed a community designed to stand disagreement, yet in order that it should exist at all, there must be some agreement regarding the place and time of its meetings, regarding the rules of procedure, and regarding some principles. In these and all similar cases, unity of judgment cannot be procured by rational communication. The believers in a social science which would, under circumstances of perfect enlightenment, eliminate the decisions of authority—and those of freedom as well—assume that the kind of necessity which makes demonstration possible extends to the particulars of social practice. But, clearly, such propositions as "It is good for us to live in this house," and "It is proper that our assembly should meet at noon," admit of no demonstration. Philosophical prejudice alone may cause failure to perceive the contingency in which such propositions are engaged. United action demands a principle that works steadily amidst the overwhelming contingencies of perishable existence. Rational communication, which is bound up with essential necessities, is not such a principle.

Does it follow that unanimity is under all circumstances an uncertain and precarious principle of unity in action? This question requires that we consider a community whose members are, without exception, ideally virtuous and enlightened persons. Unanimity is well known to be a most precarious achievement in communities afflicted by such common deficiencies as ignorance, prejudice, selfish interest, etc., but our purpose is to decide whether authority is ever needed independently of deficiencies. We must bear in mind, accordingly, a group free from stupidity and ill-will. If such a group were a Utopian fiction, it still could play a part in the understanding of society. In fact, there exist groups whose members are all intelligent and morally excellent; that these groups are very small makes no difference for the purposes of rational analysis.

RATIONAL COMMUNICATION AND AFFECTIVE COMMUNION

Since unanimity cannot be established in these practical matters by the power of demonstration, the ideally clever and virtuous members of a community cannot be unanimous in more than fortuitous fashion unless a determined course of action is demanded by the virtuous inclination of their hearts. Whenever wisdom has to find its way in the midst of circumstances contingent and possibly unique, the certainty of its judgment results from its agreement with honest inclination. An ethical issue universal in character—say, a general problem of justice

—can be answered, as St. Thomas puts it, in either of two ways, the way of cognition and the way of inclination. In the way of cognition, the answer proceeds from principles by logical connections. This is how the moral philosopher is supposed to[4] answer questions, and no other method is acceptable in philosophy, because no other method procures certainty in knowledge as knowledge. But an honest man unacquainted with deductive processes may find the answer intuitively and in incommunicable fashion by feeling that such and such a way of doing things pleases or revolts his sentiment of justice.[5] Pro-

---

[4] *Sum. Theol.* i. 1. 6 ad 3. The words "is supposed to" are not used casually. Moral philosophy is still in a rather primitive stage, and moral philosophers commonly fail to render obvious the deductive connection of their answers with the self-evident principles of the moral order. Their answers may still be true and good and worth adhering to: but the cause of their certainty is an inclination, not a deduction, and for a conclusion so attained to be safe, the philosopher's—or the theologian's—inclination must be sound, which is the same as to say that the fellow must be possessed, first, of genuine virtue and, second, of all the conditions and instruments required for the regular functioning of virtuous inclination as cause of true practical judgment. Of course whoever writes a book of ethics, whether philosophical or theological, likes the reader to believe that every bit of it is scientifically established: in case it were not, the only guaranty of his statements would be the perfection of his virtue: a thing that moralists, understandably, do not like the public to inquire into.

[5] Such words as "heart," "sentiment," etc., must not be allowed to convey the belief that the determination of the right and the wrong ever is entrusted to *emotional* reactions. Let it be said that there exist inclinations of a purely intellectual character, the best example of which is the familiarity of a man of science with the scientific field which is his; thanks to this familiarity he is able to put his finger on the true statement a long time—i.e., a few years or a few centuries—before this statement is demonstrated. The inclinations which assure the determination of the right and the wrong in contingency are not of purely intellectual nature. They pertain to the appetite and can be termed *affective* with propriety

vided his is a genuine virtue—as distinct from emotional
counterfeits—and is sufficiently developed, the judgment
dictated by such a sentiment of agreement or aversion is
certain. By love for what justice demands the heart of the
just is shaped after the pattern of justice, and his inclination is one with the requirement of his virtue. To say that
a will is virtuous is to say that its movements coincide
with the demands and aversions of virtue itself. Between
the ethically good appetite and ethical goodness there
exists a unity of nature, a connaturality, which constitutes a dependable source of practical truth. Because the
just will corresponds in all its movements to the object of
justice, the inclinations experienced by the just are like
statements uttered by the object of justice. Here, accord-

provided it is understood that the appetite of man comprises, as
its principal part, the system of desires and aversions born of rational apprehension, i.e., the will. The affective inclination which
alone can determine the right and the wrong when demonstration
is powerless is *principally* the inclination of the will, i.e., an inclination born of intelligent apprehension, and constantly strength-
ened by dedication to truth. Inclinations of an emotional character
are by no means excluded, but they are subordinated. It often is a
feeling of charm or disgust which notifies us that—perhaps in spite
of appearances—there is something definitely right or wrong about
a situation; but if such a feeling were let loose, and allowed to work
outside an integrated system whose principal part is the will, we
would run into all the absurdities of the doctrines, so popular at
the end of the eighteenth century and in the Romantic period,
which give an infrarational sentiment ultimate control over the
determination of the right and the wrong and the utterances of
reason. The "conscience" of the Savoy Vicar (J.-J. Rousseau,
Emile, III, Amsterdam, Jean Neaulme, 1762, p. 114) would not
perform any of the wonders that Rousseau describes if it were not
precisely this: an inclination antecedent to reason, more *native*
than anything born of understanding, closer to cosmical energies,
closer to animals and plants and other things of nature, and closer
to sheer existence.

ing to the words of John of St. Thomas, "Love takes on
the role of the object."[6]

It is entirely by accident that we can demonstrate so
little about the requirements of justice or chastity, considered in their intelligible universality, but it is not by
accident that nobody can demonstrate what the rule of
justice consists in under historically-conditioned, absolutely concrete, individual, and possibly unprecedented
and unrenewable circumstances. Here the rule of justice
is not uttered by an essence and cannot be grasped by the
demonstrative power of the intellect. It is uttered by the
love which is the soul of the just and it can be learned
only by listening to the teaching of love. Take for instance the problem of ownership of extreme necessity.
Our sense of justice acknowledges that a starving person,
without money and without liberal friends, has a right to
save his life with food that he cannot pay for. No doubt,
such a proposition can be demonstrated, and St. Thomas
successfully designated the middle term of its demonstration when he remarked that in case of necessity all
things become common.[7] But argumentation will never
establish a logical connection between the theory of property and the answer that *I* am looking for when, already
weakened by hunger, I wonder whether my case is actually one of extreme necessity. A man in need will know
for sure whether his necessity is extreme or not if and
only if he is so just as to feel how far the right of his
neighbor and his own right go, so temperate as not to
mistake an accidental urge for a real need, and so strong
as to fear neither the sufferings of hunger nor the resent-
ment of his illiberal neighbors.

[6] *Cursus theologicus,* i-ii. disp. 18. a. 4. Vivès, VI, p. 638.
[7] *Sum. Theol.* ii-ii. 32. 7 ad 3.

Thus, whereas a question relative to an ethical essence can be answered both by way of cognition and by way of inclination, the way of inclination alone can procure an answer when a question of human conduct involves contingency. This holds for the rules of common action as well as for those of individual conduct. Political prudence is no less dependent upon the obscure forces of the appetite than prudence in the government of individual life. However, with regard to unity of judgment among men, there is a significant difference between individual prudence and any prudence concerned with the conduct of a community. The prudence of the individual normally involves something singular and peculiar—it would almost be appropriate to say "eccentric." In their hopeless search for guidance amidst the obscurities of action, men easily assume that problems of individual conduct are the same for all, or at least for many, and that the rule which led one to a happy solution can be confidently followed by others. This assumption works sometimes, viz., when problems are not significantly modified by individual circumstances; yet it is false, and may at any time bring about disastrous effects, for, in the broad field that lies beyond determination by ethical essences, it never can be said *a priori* that individual features are irrelevant. A life of moderate work and strict parsimony may be precisely what a certain family needs, but misfortune may befall a neighboring home unless the line followed is one of rather lavish expenditure at the cost of strenuous work, and in still another case real wisdom may paradoxically require liberal spending, an abundance of leisure, and willingness to go into debt. Of such contrasting rules of action, some may prove sound in a great number of cases and some may prove harmful save for rare exceptions. Yet it is never possible to know in advance—i.e., prior to an investigation of whatever unique features a case may comprise—that the rule required in this individual case is not precisely the one which would prove unsuited to nearly all other cases. Because of the possible relevance of unique features in the determination of individual prudence, each man is threatened with the contingency of having to make his decisions in utter solitude and to act like no one else. The anguish of such solitude is more than most men can stand, hence the tendency to take refuge in uniformity and conformity, even though precious features of individual destiny may be destroyed by adherence to common practice.

When the prudence of men is concerned with the welfare of one and the same community—their community —individual features have, in principle,[8] nothing to do with the making of a wise decision. Among the most significant data, some are, indeed, strictly unique, but they pertain to the community's history and thus tend to cause agreement rather than diversity of judgment. Any common pursuit, on no matter how humble a level, is a welcome remedy to the anguished solitude of individual prudence. To be sure, science is a factor of human unity, but it is in a world of abstraction that it causes men to elicit identical judgments. In common action, alone does

[8] To see why the qualification "in principle," is necessary, consider the case of a leader who knows that, under the circumstances, he cannot resign, and that it is he, and no one else, who has to guide the community toward a certain goal. Two ways, *a* and *b,* are open; *a* would be preferable if it were not for a feature pertaining to the individual history of this leader, who cannot resign, but, his individual history being what it is, *b* ought to be preferred. In fact, whenever an individual feature modifies the ability of a leader to carry out a certain policy, this feature belongs to the system of data that *public* prudence is confronted by and has to reckon with.

concrete existence, with all its determinateness, with its character of totality, its location in time, and its contingency, tend to procure unity among men. Assuming that our community is made entirely of clever and well-intentioned persons, whatever is needed for its welfare is the object of unanimous assent. Affective communion achieves what cannot be expected of rational communication: it brings about unanimity of judgment in the life of action. Again, every certain judgment concerning what we have to do under concrete circumstances is dictated by an affective motion and owes its certain truth to its agreement with dependable inclination. But when the pursuit is that of a common good, the part played by affective and secret determinants is no longer an obstacle to unity of judgment among men. Wills properly inclined toward the same common good cannot but react in the same way to the same proposition, if what this proposition expresses is definitely what the common good demands. In groups small enough not to involve much error and bad will, the adherence of all to decisions that are necessary though indemonstrable brings about marvels of united action. As to larger communities—say, cities or nations—where all sorts of evils and deficiencies are inevitable, situations resembling unanimity and entailing most of the effects that unanimity would entail are a comparatively frequent occurrence. Consider 'the case of a nation attacked by a neighbor eager for territorial expansion. That resistance is better than appeasement cannot be demonstrated, and many citizens do not have the civic virtue which would procure indefectible adherence to what common salvation demands. Yet history shows that spontaneous unity often characterizes the reaction of peoples in this predicament. If there were a question of polling opinion, it would be impossible to speak of unanimity. There are traitors, collaborationists, neutralists, abstentionists, honest men deceived by overwhelming illusions, and passive citizens without an answer to a question that never actually reached their minds. But these disrupters of unanimity are comparatively few, and they carry so little weight as to make little difference. Practically and for all significant purposes, the situation is about what it would be if unanimity were realized.

But after having recognized the marvels that unanimity, or quasi-unanimity can work, let it be remarked that *unanimity is a precarious principle of united action whenever the common good can be attained in more than one way.* All that has been said in the foregoing about the power of unanimity simply makes no sense except when the way to the common good is uniquely determined. If the common good can be attained in more than one way, neither enlightenment nor virtue, but only chance, can bring about unanimity. Accordingly, if unity of action is guarantied by no other principle than that of unanimous agreement, it becomes an entirely casual affair, the result being either stalemate or divided and destructive action. Circumstances may be such that the happy life of a man-and-wife community can be easily attained either in Washington or in New York, but if one member of the community prefers, with the best of intentions, Washington, and the other, with an equally virtuous disposition, New York, the principle of action by unanimous agreement determines the separation of these well-meaning spouses. —There is nothing wrong with a man who so far as he is concerned, likes to drive on the right hand side of the road, and nothing wrong with the fellow who, if he had his own choice, would drive on the left. Thus traffic rules cannot be decided by the unanimous consent of enlightened and virtuous drivers. —Assuming that all good citizens are agreed that the public budget cannot be cut below such and such an amount, it is obvious that the money needed for public purposes can be gathered, without injustice or particular harm, in a diversity of ways. Citizens may, without there being anything wrong with their intelligence or intention, take diverse stands with regard to such methods of taxation as sales tax, gross income tax, or a combination of both. —In military operations, either of two plans of attack may provide a reasonable chance of victory, but defeat is certain if the attacker's power is split between the two plans. Among the most experienced and dependable leaders, some prefer one plan and some the other. There is no reason why they should be unanimous, since each plan, insofar as those things fall under human providence, is a way to victory. —Among the many ways of playing a concerto of Bach, several satisfy the requirements of great music, and highly qualified musicians will clash as to how the fourth Brandenburg Concerto should be played. Yet the members of an orchestra cannot be allowed conflicting interpretations of a concerto. In fact, any conceivable instance of common action, if considered in all its modes and particulars, admits of being carried out according to one or another of several methods, all leading to the common good.

KNOWLEDGE AND FREEDOM

To the proposition that authority, as cause of united action, exercises an essential function, i.e., a function made necessary not by any evil or deficiency but by the nature of common action, it is currently objected that any multiplicity of ways leading to a common purpose is an illusion that social science, if more developed, would dismiss. The problem involved here is that of choice, and it pertains to the subject of liberty more directly than to the subject of authority.

When the theory of liberty is not enlivened by some sort of ethical enthusiasm, it often is surrounded by a cloud of misgivings, as if liberty could be preserved only by cherished ignorance and should yield to unique determination as soon as the truth is known about the proper way to our end. Indeed, everyone's experience tells of deliberations that bear on illusory as well as genuine means. If proper information comes before decision is made, and excludes the illusory means—i.e., the lines of action which, in spite of appearances, do not lead to the end but to failure and perhaps disaster—everything is better in all conceivable respects. Considering that a wholesome simplification takes place whenever an illusory means is ruled out, we sometimes dream of carrying simplification down to the state of unique determinateness, and we like to imagine that in perfect acquaintance with the real state of affairs the lines of action originally listed as means would, with but one exception, be identified as so many illusions. It is easy to see that this postulate expresses aversion to the mystery involved in free choice as well as to the darkness of contingency. Relations characterized by sheer determinateness, without contingency and without freedom, offer an average type of intelligibility which has been constantly preferred by rationalism. Indeed, any feature of contingency is a restriction on intelligibility, but the real world may not be intelligible in all respects. It is, after all, a question of fact, and we

must be ready to accept whatever conclusion is reached
by the scientific and philosophic description of the world.
Freedom, on the other hand, if there is such a thing,
would involve extraordinary plenitude of being, causality and intelligibility. But the more intelligible is not
always the more easy to understand. In all scentific disciplines there are admirably simple views and methods
which remain inaccessible to all but a very few scholars.
Why are these things so hard to grasp? Not because they
lack intelligibility, but rather because they are so excellently intelligible that only the best intellects are propor-
tioned to them. With a mind open both to the restricted
intelligibility of things contingent and to the secrecy of
freedom, it is possible to inquire into the meaning of
choice without begging any question. Let the problem be
stated in these simple words: Is choice necessarily nar-
rowed down to one genuine and one (or several) ungenuine means? Is choice necessarily between one good
and one (or several) evils? *Is there such a thing as a choice
among goods?* Can there conceivably be several means to
an end? In a comparison of agents, should it be said that
some are restricted to one or few means and that others
have a wide variety of means at their disposal?

As soon as these questions are posed without any prejudice relative to the intelligibility of things, experience
supplies the basic answers. Several diets can maintain the
health of a healthy man, but a diseased organism may
need, as a *sine qua non* of survival, what everyone calls
a strict—i.e., uniquely determined—diet. —An ordinary student, to attain proficiency in mathematics, needs
all the complex system worked out by academic societies
—teachers, textbooks, treatises, discussions, tutorials—
but in the case of genius alternative means make it pos-

sible to dispense with much of the academic apparatus.
—It has been remarked that when a new pedagogical
method is tested by a born teacher, success proves nothing, for born teachers are known to achieve success with
almost any method; in order to know how a method is,
it is better to have it tested by an undistinguished teacher
who depends heavily on the quality of the method used.
—A man trained in one craft and unable to do any other
job often has to work in uncongenial conditions; the man
with many skills can afford to be more particular about
the circumstances of his employment. No one would say
that the broader choice open to the man with many skills
originates in ignorance and illusion; clearly, it results
from a greater power and presupposes more and better
knowledge. —An industrial enterprise with little capital
must produce only that which will surely bring immediate returns; the privilege of contributing extensively to
diversity and novelty in the market belongs to firms better financed. —It is a commonplace of American history
that waste of natural resources was determined initially
by an acute shortage of manpower. The only ways of
development open to a young community placed in
natural abundance were the wasteful ones. We judge
more severely the habits of waste in those later generations which, owing to great numbers, firmer establishment, more advanced techniques, and many other forms
of increased power, have choices that the early settlers
did not have. —A nation with no navy, a very small army,
no financial stature, and declining population, if offered
the alliance of a powerful neighbor, has to accept it albeit
at the cost of heavy sacrifices and historical resentments;
but given great bargaining power, a nation can choose
its allies. In all conceivable circumstances, power in-

creases choice. The proper effect of enlightenment, accordingly, is twofold: improved knowledge rules out illusory means and, insofar as it entails greater power, multiplies the genuine ones. To destroy the illusion of a means is not to cut the amplitude of choice, for, insofar as it extends to illusory means, choice itself is but an illusion. In an ideally enlightened community, authority would be spared the unhappy task of directing the common effort, in the darkness of illusion, along a possibly disastrous line. But, inasmuch as an excellent condition of knowledge implies greatly increased power, social science at its perfection would multiply genuine means and broaden real choice. *It would, consequently, increase the need for authority as a factor of united action in the cases where the plurality of the genuine means renders unanimity fortuitous.*

Strikingly, it is a better understanding of freedom which first discloses the essential character of the need for authority in common action. But why is it that whenever we think of diverse ways leading to the common good we are so strongly tempted to attribute their diversity, and the corresponding variety of preferences, to our ignorance of some relevant features or circumstances? A stubborn objection holds that if men were omniscient, unanimous adherence to the end would necessarily entail unanimity regarding the means. Let us briefly inquire into the causes of this belief.

In all domains of understanding and interpretation, whether trivial or lofty and subtle, we are inclined to transfer the properties of the better known subjects to subjects that are not so well known. This is why Aristotle —or some follower of his—says that it is unreasonble to seek at the same time the science of a subject and the method of this science:[9] unless the method is known in advance—albeit in the most rudimentary fashion—we shall inevitably force upon the new study dispositions acquired in previous studies, e.g., apply to medicine dispositions which proved excellent in mechanics, or consider ethics with the bias of a mind trained in theoretical science.

Notice, at this point, that the things pertaining to cognition are better known than the things pertaining to appetition and volition. Every time we turn to some aspect of appetitive and volitional life, we carry with us frames of mind and schemes of interpretation developed in our endeavor to understand cognitive life. We are inclined to reconstruct appetition after the pattern of cognition. But cognition is not free from deficiency unless it is strictly determinate. If the problem is to know what the things are, nothing is worse than perfect indifference, i.e., the state in which a proposition appears just as plausible as its contradictory. Things are somewhat better if one part of the alternative is more probable than the other, but so long as one of the two is not excluded by unqualified necessity, cognition remains defective. With regard to facts and to essences as well, the faculty of choosing, at will, between assent and dissent is not an advantage but expresses an entirely negative state of affairs. Accordingly, the understanding of cognition results in a pattern where perfection strictly coincides with uniqueness. But appetition is, in a way, the opposite of cognition, for, whereas the known is attracted into the knower, the lover is attracted toward the beloved, and whereas the true exists in the mind, the good

9 *Met.* 2.3. 995a13. That the treatise classified as Bk. 2 (α) of *Metaphysics* was written by Aristotle himself is questioned by some.

exists in the things.[10] This basic contrast reverses the meaning of uniqueness, plurality and indifference, when inquiry moves from cognition to appetition. A plurality of possible assents with regard to one and the same subject evidences failure to attain truth with certainty; the indifference of the uncertain mind is made of inachievement, indetermination, potentiality, passivity. On the contrary, a plurality of means with regard to one and the same end evidences mastery, domination, actuality, activity, superdetermination. The myth of a perfect knowledge which would eliminate authority and liberty rests upon a crude confusion of two kinds of indifference: the passive one, which results from potency and inachievement, and the dominating one, which results from excellence.

An Essential Function of Authority

The existence of a plurality of genuine means in the pursuit of the common good excludes unanimity as a *sufficient* method of steadily procuring unity of action. To achieve indispensable unity in common action, one method is left, which can be described as follows: whether we prefer to live in Washington or in New York, whether we prefer to drive on the right or on the left side of the road, whether we prefer sales tax, gross income tax, or their combination, whether we prefer a richer or a more austere orchestration of Bach, everyone of us, insofar as he is engaged in the common action, will accept and follow, as rule of his own action, one judgment thus constituted into rule for all. This rule of common action may coincide with my own preference, but this is of no significance, for the common rule might just as well be

[10] *Met.* 6.4. 1027b25.

at variance with my liking, and I would be equally bound to follow it out of dedication to the common good, which cannot be attained except through united action. *The power in charge of unifying common action through rules binding for all is what everyone calls authority.*[11]

[11] Between the concept of authority and that of law there exist enlightening relations. It is, indeed, perfectly proper to speak of the authority of the legislator, and nothing would warrant the identification of authority with executive power. Many acts of authority assume the form of laws passed by assemblies. However, authority and law evidence opposite intelligible tendencies inasmuch as the more a proposition is expressive of necessity, the more it participates—other things being equal—in the character of law, whereas there is nothing, in the concept of authority, that expresses aversion to contingency. A law rules human acts in the capacity of premise, not of conclusion; now, the more a premise is independent of contingency, the more of a premise it is. The first or absolute premises regulating human actions express the absolute necessities intelligibly following upon the rational nature. But authority is perfectly at home in the management of contingency and in the uttering of practical conclusions. A decree which applies a law to a particular and unique situation is no less an act of authority than a law passed by an assembly to establish a principle that can be applied to indefinitely many particular situations. No doubt, this law is already so particularized, and so engaged in contingency as not to be a sheer expression of natural necessity. Yet it retains the character of premise, and calls for further determination in terms of adjustment to contingencies that an assembly cannot deal with. Common usage contrasts "government by law" and "authoritarian government." Both of these expressions are objectionable, and their meaning has to be carefully specified. In a way every government is authoritarian. On the other hand, "government by law" conveys the suggestion that propositions retaining the character of premises may suffice to guide a community in entirely concrete and perhaps unique situations, and this involves the nonsense of a premise which is also an ultimate conclusion. Provided these abusive interpretations are definitely ruled out, it is perfectly correct to use the expression "government by law" when a political system depends as much as possible on premises established by the wisdom of the legislator, and to call "authoritarian" the system of government which gives the few men in the executive power the

It may be a distinct person designated by nature, as in the couple and in the family. It may be a distinct person designated by God, as in the cases of Saul and Peter. It may be a distinct person designated by the people, as in the case of David. It may be a distinct person designated by birth and accepted by the people. It may be a distinct group of persons designated by heredity or by election or by lot. And it may be no distinct person or group of persons, but the community itself proceeding by majority vote. The problem of the need for authority and the problem of the need for a distinct governing personnel have often been confused: at this point, it is already clear that they are distinct and that the argumentation which establishes the need for authority, even in a society made of ideally enlightened and well-intentioned persons, leaves open the question of whether some communities may be provided with all the authority they need without there being among them any distinct group of governing persons.

Thus, authority does not have only substitutional functions; in other words, it is not made necessary by deficiencies alone. We know, by now, that in one case at least the need for authority derives not from any lack or privation but from the sound nature of things. Given a community on its way to its common good, and given, on the part of this community, the degree of excellence which entails the possibility of attaining the good in a diversity of ways, authority has an indispensable role to play, and this role originates entirely in plenitude and

---

greatest possible liberty to manage the concrete circumstances by connecting the conclusions of their choice with premises that have no other source than their good judgment, since no positive enactment ever gave these premises any juridical existence.

accomplishment. The deficiency theory of authority is given the lie. An ideally enlightened and virtuous community needs authority to unify its action. By accident, it may need it less than a community which, as a result of ignorance, is often confronted by illusory means. But by essence it is more powerful than any community afflicted with vice and ignorance, and as a result of its greater power it controls choices involving new problems of unity which cannot be solved by way of unanimity but only by way of authority.

THE FORM AND THE MATTER OF THE COMMON GOOD

Engaged in the pursuit of a common end, we deliberate about ways of insuring the unity of our action. These may be the steady ways of authority or, should it prove impossible to embody the principle of authority in an appropriate agency, the precarious ways of unanimity. But the problem would not arise if we were not already intending in common a certain end. Underlying any problem relative to the unity of common action, there exist problems relative to the end of the action to be united. The next step in the theory of authority concerns the end willed in common, as presupposed by the question of the way to unify action toward this end. Let this problem be posed as follows: granted that authority has an essential part to play in the unifying of action toward the common end, does it have any essential part to play with regard to the common end itself?

The precise vocabulary worked out by Aristotle (*Ethics.* 3.) and improved by Aquinas (i-ii, 6ff.) can supply much valuable clarity. In perfect accord with the best usage of common language, philosophers describe "volition" as the act by which the will adheres to its end. If the end is considered, not absolutely as a thing good to attain, but more precisely as term of a means or series of means, the act of the will is called "intention." "Choice" deals with a diversity of means relative to the thing intended and willed. Thus, after having established that authority has an essential function in the order of choice and means, we are asking whether it has, by reason of the nature of things and not merely by accident, anything to do with the volition and the intention of the common good explicitly considered as an end.

To say the least, appearances strongly suggest that any function of authority concerned with the end is merely substitutional. It looks very much as if, in a community made exclusively of enlightened and virtuous persons, the volition and intention of the common good should be fully insured by the qualities of the persons. Whoever disregards the common good is not virtuous but selfish, and whoever is dedicated to genuine virtue is, by the very efficacy of his virtue, ready for any sacrifice that the common good demands. It seems that ideally enlightened and virtuous persons would be adequately related to the good of their community by their enlightened virtue. In societies such as the cities and states of our experience, where selfishness and ignorance prevail, persons have to be constantly directed and often coerced toward the common good. Men of ill will seek their own advantage and ignore the good of all, and many whose will is honest and even generous happen to place the character of common good where it does not belong. But suppose that both ill will and error are removed; the need for authority, insofar as the common good itself is concerned, seems to disappear. Authority, in an ideal community, would have no essential function, except with regard to the unity of common action when there exists a plurality of genuine means.

It sometimes happens that a very simple analysis suffices to bring into focus difficulties hidden by familiar appearances. In a discussion of authority with regard to the *end* of common action, it is decisively important to bear in mind the meaning of the polar opposition between form and content within the object of volition and intention. Consider this object, i.e., the end willed (as a thing absolutely good) and intended (as a term of means). It can be willed and intended in two ways. I may will and intend what is good without knowing *what the thing is* that is good. The daily life of a man of good will is made of problems of content stated on the basis of a satisfactory answer to a problem of form. The man of good will, by definition and hypothesis, wills that which is good, and firmly adheres to the form of goodness. If only he knew *what the thing is* in which the form of goodness resides, he would do the good thing and all would be perfect. There is an evil harmony in the sinful will which adheres to evil things known to be evil—i.e., known to bear the form of evil[12]—and there is a blessed harmony in the good will which, for the sake of goodness, adheres to things that are actually good. And between these two harmonies there is the daily problem of the man of good will who indeed adheres to the form of the good but feels uncertain about the thing in which this form resides, in other words, the matter or content of this form.

So far as community life is concerned, the problem of matter and form within the end can be posed as follows:

---

[12] Evil is a privation, not a form, but this privation is understood after the pattern of a form and cannot be understood otherwise.

Is it desirable that the common good be willed and intended, both with regard to matter and with regard to
form, by private persons acting in a private capacity? In
order to be sure that we reach the root of the issue, let
us consider the case of a society with no distinct governing personnel. Here are a few hundred farmers who
gather periodically into a people's assembly, and this
assembly is the only government of their community.
Assuming that the order of virtuous intention obtains, I
recognize in each farmer a dual capacity. Between the
sessions of the assembly, he is Philip or Bartholomew, a
private person, the husband of Ruth or Patricia, the
father of these children, and the owner of this particular
land unmistakably distinguished by a fence from the rest
of the world. His duties are unique. A good neighbor
and companion, he wants all fields to bear abundantly;
yet he is responsible, in a unique way, for the plowing of
the field described as his. A good-hearted man, he is
ready to help any child that God places in his path, yet
there would be dire subversion of order if he did not
show special dedication to the children who are his, and
prefer them, in intention and in action, to other children
who, though equally lovely, are not in equal degree entrusted to his love.[13] In the relation of man and wife, a

[13] According to a well-known remark of Aristotle, the natural
order of excellence may be reversed by a condition of emergency.
To philosophize is, absolutely speaking, better than to make
money; but for the fellow who is in dire poverty, to get money is
better than to philosophize. Likewise, the order of love which requires that, under ordinary circumstances, I should provide my
own children with advantages that many other children do not
have, also requires that in an emergency—e.g., flood, epidemic,
war, revolution—I should deprive my own people of goods that are
not needed for their survival in order to insure the survival of
children who are not mine.

dedication unique in all respects is the essence of indissoluble marriage.

When the assembly meets, every citizen is expected to assume a new capacity. A man who yesterday was admired for his industry on his family farm would today be blamed if his devotion did not belong entirely to the community. Between the private and the common welfare, the relation is often one of harmony. But conflicts may arise at any time and a public person, say, a member of the people's assembly, is bound to uphold the public welfare, regardless of how his private interest is affected. For instance, a certain method of taxation, plainly beneficial to the community as a whole, may cause serious difficulty to the kind of enterprise that he is managing. If a member of a people's assembly is known to have opposed a beneficial taxation law for no other reason than the threat of increased difficulty for his own enterprise, we consider him, according to the seriousness of the circumstances, either a weak person or a despicably bad citizen. At any rate, this accident of private interest interfering with public service in the discharge of a public function is inconceivable in the community of virtuous and enlightened persons which remains the principal subject of our inquiry. Considering, thus, the citizen of a direct democracy who, by the very fact that there is no distinct governing personnel, is the bearer of two capacities— the public and the private, according as the people's assembly is or is not in session—and assuming, further, that this person acts blamelessly in each capacity, I recognize what difference there is between these two relations.

The problem would certainly be overlooked if we were

satisfied with the contrast between the private and the common. Again, this virtuous citizen is dedicated to the common good at all times, whether or not the assembly is in session, and, unmistakably, the difference that we are trying to express concerns, not the common good and its opposite, but two relations to the common good. The private person, inasmuch as he is morally excellent, wills and intends the common good, and subordinates his private wishes to it. He may not know what action the common good demands, but he adheres to the common good formally understood, to the form of the common good, whatever may be the matter in which this form resides; as far as content or matter is concerned, it is his business to will and intend private goods. But the public person is defined by the duty of willing and intending the common good considered both in its form and in its matter. And because the service of the common good normally involves an arrangement of things private, and sometimes requires the sacrifice of private interests, the subject of the public capacity exercises authority over the private person, whose business it is to look after par-ticular matters.

In spite of appearances, the essence of authority and that of obedience are integrally preserved in a community practicing government by majority vote without any distinct governing personnel. The decisive question is not whether the content or matter of the common good is entrusted to distinct persons; it is whether, by reason of the common good's primacy, the volition and inten-tion of *that in which* the common good resides must be expressed by a rule of action binding on all. The citizens of a direct democracy are inclined to boast of having no other masters than themselves.[14] This attitude may mean merely that they like to do without a distinct governing personnel. But the same boastful words may express the will to eliminate, through constitutional contrivance, the essence of authority and that of obedience. The soul of the system is revealed by the interpretation of majority, minority, and opposition. A citizen who, whenever the assembly meets, finds himself in the majority, may believe that he obeys only himself. How is he going to feel when the majority votes against his preference? If he considers that the law he voted against is just as obligatory, and for the same reasons, as any law that he voted for, he is a law-abiding and obedient citizen for whom personal preference is altogether accidental. But if a person considers himself free from obligation to a law which he opposed, we understand that he has always been a rebel. True, he gave no signs of rebellion so long as the law was to his liking; but his later attitude discloses that having his own way has always been for him the thing essential, and obedience to the law a mere appearance.

[14] There are, in the history of mankind, only a few communities governed exclusively by the methods of direct democracy. But every democracy, no matter how important the part that a distinct personnel plays in its operation, embodies direct democracy in some of its political processes. These processes may either pertain to the written constitution, e.g., plebiscite, or to the unwritten one, e.g., the influence of public opinion. In all cases the citizens of a democracy are tempted to boast of having no masters except themselves, for they truly exercise much political power besides the electing of their leaders. The United States Constitution mentions two assemblies: the House and the Senate. There is a third one which does not need to be mentioned because its existence is obvious and which could hardly be mentioned in a written document, because of the indefiniteness of its role and power: it is the People of the United States.

THE MOST ESSENTIAL FUNCTION OF AUTHORITY

Thus, bringing about unity in common action is not, among the functions of authority, the only one which should be described as essential. Again, the problem of how to unify action—whether by unanimity or by authority—arises only on the ground of an already determinate volition and intention of the common good. Such volition and intention involve an antecedent function of authority, and this function, inasmuch as it is relative to the very end of common action, is more essential than anything pertaining to means. *The most essential function of authority is the issuance and carrying out of rules expressing the requirements of the common good considered materially.*

This theory implies that two capacities are normally and desirably distinguished in every community. With reference to the best known case, i.e., that of the body politic versus its components—individuals, families, etc. —these capacities have been called public and private. But in the present inquiry they should rather, by the rule of strict appropriateness, be designated as common and particular. Indeed, the capacity thus far called public exists in all communities, whether actually public, like a township, a county, and a state, or private, like a family. On the other hand, we shall soon see that the basic opposition is not between the common and the private but, more precisely, between the common and the particular: for privateness is but one mode of particularity. *The common capacity is defined by a relation to the common good considered not only in its form but also in its matter or content.* As to the particular capacity, it involves a relation to the form of the common good but not to its matter. Clearly, if the particular capacity were related to both the form and the matter of the common good, it would cease to be particular; the problem of authority would disappear, as far at least as the volition and intention of the common good are concerned. The whole theory stands or falls upon the answer to this simple question: Is it desirable that there should exist, in every community, persons whose business it is, within the order of material consideration, to look after goods particular rather than after the common good?[15] It almost irresistibly seems that a disposition concerned with the form of the common good but not with its matter is just about half of a virtue. A person determined to serve the common good but unconcerned with the matter of its requirements seems to stop half way, and it looks very much as if a "full measure of devotion" would extend to the matter of the common good as well as to its form.

Let us refer, once more, to a community governed by majority vote. According to a project under deliberation, a certain road, so far a very quiet one, would be paved and opened to fast-moving traffic. Large families live on this road, and the parents are worried about increased danger to their children. But, in spite of the risk involved, the good of the community demands that the road should be paved, and worried fathers, acting as members of the

[15] Once more, we are not asking whether society necessarily ought to be divided into two groups of persons, viz., a distinct governing personnel, and the governed. When we speak of "persons whose business it is . . . to look after particular goods, ..." we do not exclude the possibility that all these persons should, in another capacity, constitute the agency in charge of looking after the common good.

people's assembly, support the project. By the terms of
the preceding description, these good citizens, exercis-
ing the capacity of particular persons between the sessions
of the assembly, should oppose the project as dangerous
to their children, with a firm determination, however, to
abide by the decision of the majority. Here, the twofold
capacity described in the foregoing seems irrelevant.
These citizens, though lovingly concerned with danger
to their children, will and intend the form of the common
good. Consequently, they refrain from any rebellious act
against the decision to pave the road, although they do
their best under all circumstances to reduce the danger.
*If these good people can do so much, why should they
not do a little more* and, without waiting for the emergence of a new capacity at the assembly's session, confess
that the road should be paved? The construct of a community made of ideally enlightened and virtuous persons seems to imply, over and above adherence to the
common good formally considered, the determinate volition of the things that the common good actually requires or contains. But then, the volition and intention
of the common good, both with regard to form and with
regard to matter, are adequately guaranteed by enlightened virtue. As far, at least, as the volition and intention
of the common good are concerned, an ideally perfect
community seems able to do without authority.

Thus, according to a plausible hypothesis, the perfection of virtue causes the capacity described as particular
to disappear into the common capacity. A single capacity
is left, which is altogether relative to the common good.
*The particular capacity, by taking in hand the matter of
the common good, has indeed become common.* Such

transmutation is precisely what was suggested when we voiced the conjecture that excellent citizens, fully prepared to make all sacrifices required by the common good, should take one more step and, without assuming any new capacity, should will and intend the common good materially considered. *It remains to be decided how the common good itself is affected by the disappearance or impairment of the particular capacity.*

THE FUNCTION AND THE SUBJECT

Let us first analyze particularity into its main types. Every community exercises several functions—e.g., in the case of the state, justice, defense, diplomacy, public works, etc.—and in relation to the whole life of the community each function obviously has the character of a part. But in what specific sense does the notion of particularity apply here? Take, for instance, national defense. It is aimed at protecting all the national territory, all its wealth, all its counties, townships, families, and citizens. This function is altogether relative to the common good, yet it retains the character of a part inasmuch as its object is not the total good of the community but only one aspect of it. The object of a function is a certain aspect of a whole, and this is what defines particularity in the case of the function. The subject whose good is sought may be an individual organism—indeed the concept of function is basic in biology; it may be a person, and it may just as well be a community of any rank and description. Whether the subject considered is an organism, a person or a community, the successful exercise of one function is only an aspect and a part of its good condition; if other functions are defective, disaster is not ruled out. A function may be public in an unqualified sense, as in the case of the functions pertaining exclusively to the body politic, without ceasing to be particular, inasmuch as its object is but one aspect of a complex good.

In sharp contrast to the particularity of the function, a good may be particular by reason of its subject. Consider the activities involved in the upbringing of a child: taken together, they intend the whole good of the child, not one aspect of it. But because the child is part of the community, his is a particular good. Private communities, as the family, and such public communities as the township, the county, and the units of a federal organization are also related to the larger communities of which they are members as particular subjects. The state is the community which is so complete and self-sufficient that its good is not that of a particular subject—individual, family, township, etc.—but, unqualifiedly, the common good of men assembled for the sake of noble life.[16]

Let us now examine the question of the excellence of the particular in the two ways of particularity just defined. Familiar experiences suffice to show how desirable it is that functions should be clearly distinguished, and that each of them should be exercised with a special eag-

[16] If the word state is supposed to designate the most complete temporal society, the questions "Where is the center of the state" and "What are the boundaries of the state" may raise difficulties in federal organizations. In the American Union, for instance, it may be wondered whether the philosophic essence of the state is found in each of the fifty component units, or in the Federal Union itself. Where is the center of the "complete temporal community" to which a Canadian citizens belongs? Is it the capital of the province, that of the Dominion or that of the Commonwealth? The answer to such questions may not be unanimous. Whether it is or not, it is not determined exclusively by constitutional law, but also by history, and it may change without any change occurring in the letter of the constitutions.

erness for what is unique about it. It is good for the community that military men be devoted with a passion to national defense, bridge builders to the building of bridges, foresters to the preservation of forests, physicians to public health, and classicists to the study of the classics. The particularity of the function removes confusion and opens the way to the advantages of specialization. It is hardly possible that both the task of building bridges and that of conserving forests should be successfully fulfilled by the same persons; but even if a team happened to be expert both in bridge building and in forestry, a division of social labor would still be necessary with regard to place and time. One reason why we keep rereading the *Republic* of Plato is that it expresses better than any other book the ideal of a community from which confusion is removed, and in which justice is achieved, through wise division of labor and dedication to specific tasks. A most enjoyable clarity pertains to the distinctness of the function, for every function is relative to an object, and, in human affairs at least, every object is definable. When the object of a social function no longer can be defined, the function itself becomes meaningless: this is when reformers step in. The administration of justice, the conduct of foreign relations, the management of public finances, etc., are so many functions defined by perfectly intelligible objects.

Since functions are concerned with distinct aspects of the common good, functional diversity causes a need for an agency relative to the common good as a whole. Bringing about order among functions is the job of this central agency. What ratio of public funds can be allocated to agricultural projects without jeopardizing national defense or public health? This is an issue on which the function of promoting agriculture, the function of defending the national territory and the function of procuring good health conditions have nothing to say, except in purely preparatory and indecisive fashion. Decision pertains to a power which, inasmuch as it is responsible for order among the functions, necessarily controls all of them and commands all the functionaries.

The particularity of the function, as ground of authority, has a negative feature of major significance: it does not, in any essential manner, set limits to the authority that it grounds. In fact, authority is commonly restricted, and often crippled, by the resistance of its functionaries: but this is an entirely accidental occurrence. Such resistance is foreign and opposed to the concept of function. True, it may be held desirable that functionaries be possessed of some autonomy, and it may be a matter of fact that they always are. But their autonomy is caused by a particularity which is not that of the function. This simple remark sums up many products of political theory as well as many facts pertaining to the history of government. Because the functionary, as such, is an instrument, the particularity of the function is a thing that despots do not dread. They know that, all other things being equal, the clear division of social labor into functions increases the efficacy of their power.

Let us now ask whether the particularity of the subject possesses an excellence of its own. No doubt, it helps to remove confusion. A good way to make sure that every farmer knows what piece of land he is supposed to till is to divide the land into homesteads. This is indeed a result of considerable value, and it may constitute an everlasting argument in favor of private ownership. However, the power of removing confusion does not belong to the particularity of the subject in strict appropriateness, since it also belongs to the particularity of the function. A factory where rigorous discipline obtains and whose workers, for the most part, can be easily replaced, has but minimum recourse to the particularity of the subject. The feats of order accomplished by the modern organization of industry have given a new appeal to the old ideal of a state which would keep free from confusion without releasing the suspicious energies of such powers as privately owned land, privately conducted schools, strongly organized families, and citizens protected by inalienable rights.

The decisive fact is that the particularity of the subject, in all its forms and degrees, involves antonomy. To use a simple example, let us imagine that all the parts of a vast plain, by reason of homogeneity in all relevant respects, produce the same crops. Within such functional unity, farming can be administered according to the diversity of the tasks (plowing, fertilizing, sowing, etc.); then it is a public affair, entrusted, say, to a branch of the Department of Agriculture. But the cultivation of this plain can also be entrusted to a multiplicity of farms each of which is governed by its individual proprietor. For the comparison to be meaningful, we must, of course, assume that other things are equal. Under definite circumstances, one system of management may insure a much higher yield than the other. In the assumption that the production is about the same in either system, let us ask whether it is better that the job be done by a multitude of self-ruling agents or by mere instruments of a central agency.

To ask this question is like asking whether there is more perfection in life than in lifelessness, in activity than in mere instrumentality, in plenitude than in emptiness.

Clearly, a whole is better off if its parts are full of initiative than if they are merely traversed by an energy which never becomes their own. Much can be learned from the fact that social thinkers and metaphysicians conduct, on the subject of plenitude versus vacuum, parallel dialogues. The book of William James, *A Pluralistic Universe,* forcefully expresses the metaphysical sentiment that genuine plurality, in the world of our experience, is the condition of meaning and plenitude. A totality which does not admit of autonomous parts disappears into the vacuum caused by its imperialistic arrogance. But the particularity of the subject, in the social as well as in the metaphysical world, harbors mysteries that are extremely uncongenial to the rationalistic mind. Whenever it has its own way in social affairs, rationalism exalts the clarity of the function and crushes the particularity of the subject.

To be sure, choice and contingency often make it impossible to explain the distinction between communities of the same functional type. What reasons could we bring forth if we had to say why two states or nations remain separated by a borderline instead of merging into one unit? The notion of natural boundary is not absurd, and sometimes a fence built by nature serves quite reasonably to distinguish one community from another. Spain is south of the Pyrenees Range and France north of it. But in many other cases, the most famous of which is the great East European plain, nations remain stubbornly distinct although they cannot claim any natural boundary. Sometimes language supplies reasonable principles of unity and diversity, but it also happens that peoples refuse to merge in spite of linguistic unity (e.g., the French-speaking Swiss and Belgians do not want to be one nation with the French) and it also happens that the unity of a nation (e.g., Switzerland) is in no way jeopardized by diversity of language. After having probed all such causes of unity and diversity, we must confess that the final power of determination belongs to the choices of men and to the accidents of history. Whatever is accidental is, as such, unexplainable, but in the world of action a thing can be significant, worthy, treasurable, without having any character of essentiality or intelligibility: it just is, it has been, it tends to keep being, and this is why it is significant, without any further explanation. The precise location of the borderline between Canada and the United States is, in a number of places, entirely conventional, but by the decision of history the community centered about Ottawa is something else than the community centered about Washington, D.C. Again, there may be no good reason why the borderline between Colorado and New Mexico should be where it is rather than a few miles farther north or farther south. Yet it is hardly questionable that the community whose main centers are Colorado Springs and Denver is, by the decisions of history, different from the community whose main centers are Santa Fe and Albuquerque. Any rationalist, if in the position of philosopher-king, would erase the borderline between Colorado and New Mexico and reduce the fifty States to a smaller number of more rational units. Such operations, which would sweep away a great deal of mystery, would also destroy much historical substance and, in a number of cases, leave only deceptive clarity where there used to be historical plenitude. No doubt, existent particularities may be dead remnants and their suppression may prove beneficial. But it also happens that the works of the past, no matter how contingent, are so full of life that their disappearance would involve great destruction. In a profound sense a "survival" is a thing which maintains in the present some of the life which was that of the past. Such life is not clearly intelligible, for an important part of it results from the successful management of contingent occurrences over a long time.

THE PERSON

It is in the individual subject of human existence that we can best observe the relation between the mysteries of contingency and those of free choice. As a member of a species, distinguished within the species by the material components of his being, a human subject is more properly designated as an individual. Considered as a complete substance which owes to its rationality a unique way of being a whole and of facing the rest of the universe, he is more properly designated as a person. The fortune of "personalism" in the ideologies of our time is clearly traceable to the promises held by the notion of person, as distinct from that of individual, in the working out of difficulties which, though of all times, have assumed extraordinary significance in the last generations. Indeed, the word personalism often stood for doctrines and attitudes that "individualism" would designate with equal or greater accuracy. Such a confusing change in expression bears witness to the power that the idea of person came to possess in minds confronted by problems which, some time before, were not held so obvious and momentous. Many, who would have been satisfied with the language of individualism half a century ago, were necessitated by the spirit of the age to speak a personalistic language. But what is it that caused, in such a large variety of doctrinal contexts, the decline of individualistic rhetoric, and a new attention to the meaning of the person? With due allowance for profound diversities among the so-called personalistic schools of thought, it can be said that the displacement of "individualism" by "personalism" generally expressed the following insights:

(1) As recalled in the foregoing, the philosophy of individualism implies that whatever is called common good is merely useful, that things common are but means, and that the character of end belongs exclusively to the individual. "Means" and "end" must be understood here rigorously: a mere means is a thing which has no desirability of its own and which would not be desired at all if it did not lead to a thing desirable in its own right. The mere means, in other words, the thing that is merely useful, is just traversed by the goodness of the end. To treat the common good as a thing merely useful becomes the *critical* periods, but as soon as the possibility of a new *organic* period[17] is strongly felt, to represent the common good as sheer utility without any dignity of its own is

---

[17] These Saint-Simonian expressions [*Exposition de la doctrine de Saint-Simon,* ed. by Elie Halévy and C. Bouglé (Paris: Rivière, 1924), p. 127] are used here without the connotations implied by the Saint-Simonian philosophy of historical causality. For the Saint-Simonists, the great facts of change as well as the great facts of permanence in human history are determined by ideas, and especially by religious beliefs. Accordingly an organic period is defined as one "in which all the facts of human activity are classified, foreseen, and set in order by a general theory, and in which the goal of social action is clearly defined." A critical period is one "in which all communion of thought, all common action, all coordination have ceased to exist, and in which society has become nothing else than an aggregation of isolated individuals fighting against each other." The distinction between organic and critical periods remains meaningful without deciding whether the organic and the critical character are due to beliefs or to factors of another kind, or to a diversity of factors including beliefs.

unbearably paradoxical. Only the pressures and appeals
of a critical period can make men blind to the character
of the common good as an autonomous good, *bonum
honestum,* and to the primacy that it enjoys as long as
the common and the particular are contained within the
same order. When such pressures and appeals have become things of the past, the sense for the eternal worth
of the human individual is not necessarily weakened, but
why should we keep using the language and the ways of a
philosophy committed to treating the common good as a
thing with no excellence of its own?

(2) Another aspect of classical individualism concerns
the role of material causality in human affairs. The features involved belong both to economic and political
theory. The individualism of the economists proceeds,
in part, from the stubborn belief that the best state of
affairs is brought about by the independent operation of
ultimate units, viz., the independent money-maker, the
individual supplier of labor-force, the individual con-
sumer, the individual organizer, etc., all moved by the
power of individual well-being. Likewise, some democratic polities embody the postulate that what is best for
the state is steadily brought about by the solitary determination of its individual components. These polities,
famously associated with the teaching of Rousseau and
with Jacobinism, strive to maintain the isolation of the
citizen. The best state would emerge from the sheer
multitude of its citizens and be confronted by nothing
but such a multitude. Again, we are dealing here with a
disposition marked by the characteristics of the critical
periods.

The use of the word *organic,* as in "organic period,"
suffices to conjure up the danger of attributing to society

a unity of *primary* character. Likening society to an organism may be useful as long as we remain in control of our analogies and understand that society is not one after the fashion of an organic body. Its individual members are not organs or cells but primary subjects of human existence. What we need is a concept expressive of the unique way in which an individual exercises membership in a set when the set is a community of intelligent beings. This concept is that of person rather than that of individual. True, the person is sociable by essence and it is capable of playing the role of part (the persons who make up the Senate are parts of the Senate), and the individual, inasmuch as it is a thing "undivided in itself and divided from all the rest,"[18] implies a character of wholeness and separation. But when the being which is an individual and a person is considered *as member of a set* (and this is the relevant way of considering it in the theory of society, for the unity of society is that of an ordered set), the concept of person restricts the character of part whereas the concept of individual expresses no such restriction. *As member of a set* the individual is purely and simply a part. But because personality, in every possible connection, expresses a universe of reason and freedom, emphasis on the person implies emphasis on the privileges of this universe. In its most intelligent forms at least, personalism, with all its ambiguities, had the merit of tracing to the unique kind of totality which results from rationality and liberty effects that the individualism of the critical period used to trace to the spontaneity of the part. If atoms were persons, their arrangements would account for many wonders that Epicurean imagination leaves unaccounted for.

[18] *Sum. Theol.,* i.29.4.

(3) Above all, the autonomy of the individual man, as fact of nature and as moral requirement, is incomparably better expressed by the notion of person than by that of individual.[19] Just as it is desirable, in all respects and most precisely in relation to the common good, that the affairs of the state be not managed by the federal power but by the state itself, and the affairs of the county by the county, and the affairs of the township by the township, and the affairs of the family by the family, so it is ultimately desirable that the affairs of the individual man, as long as he is free from important deficiency, be managed by himself. But when the individual man is precisely considered as a being possessed of integrity and rationality, when he is considered as an agent in control of his destiny, when he is considered as an agent which contains its own law not merely by way of natural constitution, but also and principally by way of understanding, voluntariness and freedom, the aspect brought forth is that of personality. On the level of individual existence, autonomy belongs to the person more properly than to the individual. Such greater propriety makes much difference both in terms of explanation and in terms of appeal. The most

[19] When individuation originates in matter, as it does in all composite substances, man included, to speak of the "autonomy of the individual" involves a degree of inappropriateness. To be sure, individuals are possessed of autonomy, but the principle of their autonomy is not the same as the principle of their individuality. Matter is that which has no law of its own. In a composite substance all that has the character of a law comes from the form. But the form is specific and consequently all the law of the material individual is the law of its species. In order to reach the principle of a norm concerned with what is unique in the individual substance, we have to turn to the concept which results from the union of *completeness* in substantial constitution and *rationality* in specific nature: this is, by the celebrated definition of Boethius, the concept of person.

valuable contribution of personalism is the general theory that the particularity of the human individual, in ultimate contradistinction to that of the function, is a privilege of personality.

Indeed, it is historically absurd to speak of personalism in the singular, as if the various personalistic movements were possessed of doctrinal unity. Endless variety is found in the positive content of their programs, and, whereas each of them is marked by sharp opposition to some general feature of the modern world, the objects of their oppositions may not coincide and may even contrast with each other. Yet there is more unity in the aversions of the personalists than in their assertions, and of all their aversions the most steady concerns the predominance of function in the order of society. If the use of one word to designate such a variety of doctrines, attitudes, inspirations and moods can be justified at all, it should be justified by the central significance, in all personalistic movements, of the conflict between person and function.

THE SUBJECT AND THE PERSON

Thus, in terms of most essential necessity, authority is needed because it is desirable that particular goods should be taken care of by particular agencies. Some of these agencies are defined by their functions, others are constituted by subjects of various kinds. Along the line which goes from the broader to the more narrow, a particular subject may be a state in a federal union, a county in a state, a township in a county, a family in a township. The ultimateness of the individual is accompanied by the emergence of significant features: this whole, the individual man, is possessed of substantial unity, whereas the other subjects, state, township, family, are not. And by reason of its rational nature, this whole, the individual man, is, in a way, all things, adheres to the absoluteness of the good, and thereby achieves mastery over its own acts. Extreme amplitude arises just when the most narrow unit is attained, for it is not in a merely metaphorical sense that a complete substance of rational nature is said to be a universe. As soon as this is understood, a new light is shed on the particularity of the antecedent subjects. A family, for instance, is not just a smaller group within a township: each of its members is all things; a family is a whole made of universes, each of which is in control of its own operations—a perfection that no solar system can achieve. Owing to the unique character of totality which belongs to the individual substance of rational nature, the whole system of the subjects is transfigured: a family, a township, a county are particular subjects, they are particular after the fashion of the subject, they are parts indeed, but of these parts the ultimate components are wholes which in a way comprehend all things. At all levels of human association the presence of the person causes the energies of totality and liberty to be present.

Looking again at the series of the particular subjects, but from the opposite standpoint, let us now remark that the most particular of them, the person, comes to exist, by virtue of its own sociability, in subjects that are less and less particular, up to the level of a community describable as complete.[20] With regard to the social character of the person, much confusion would be spared if some attention were given to the difference between (1) sociability

[20] It is obvious that no human community is unqualifiedly complete, but insofar as the most comprehensive of our communities remains incomplete, we keep struggling toward something beyond the least incomplete of the existent communities.

as such and (2) the tendency to exist in a society as a part in a whole. To be sure, the notion of person expresses wholeness and opposes the character of part, just as the notion of freedom expresses dominating indifference and opposes contingency, and just as the notion of being expresses actuality and opposes potency. But just as finite being cannot exist without an admixture of potency, and just as our freedom cannot exist without harboring some amount of passive indifference, so the person of man, by reason of all the limitations which place it at an infinite distance from absolute personality, demands to exist in a community as a part in a whole. Yet certain features of sociability belong to the human person *qua* person, and in all the system of human relations, nothing is more determining, more decisive, more distinguishing and more final than the acts traceable to the sociability of the person considered as such. In the small area of concentrated energy where these acts take place, the disinterestedness of tendencies and the other-centeredness of needs are more than facts of nature: they involve a commitment of the self in its distinct existence. No doubt, disinterested tendencies and other-centered needs are present in animals, but so long as the reason is not at work the individual agent contributes only a tendency toward its own satisfaction. Disinterestedness and other-centeredness are contributed by nature; in other words, they are caused by a dynamism antecedent to individual activity. The experience of human disorder shows that a tendency which, by nature, is disinterested and which, in fact, serves another subject, may involve no generosity on the part of the agent. Thus, some mothers love their children in a selfish way; out of selfish love they would do many things beneficial to the child, expose themselves to great dangers and inflict upon themselves great sacrifices. Here, other-centered needs are satisfied and some acts demanded by disinterested tendencies are elicited. But the way of acting remains interested and self-centered. Effects of generous love are brought into existence without generosity. Much is given, and yet action does not *proceed by way of gift.* When the devotion of a mother to her child bears these characteristics, it is commonly interpreted as an animal passion, and thereby we mean that it is nature —that is, a dynamism antecedent to reason and voluntariness—which places the effect of love in another rather than in the acting self. It is only where reason, voluntariness, and free choice are at work that the subject takes care of transcending its subjectivity: then actions that are gifts also *proceed by way of gift.* Such disinterestedness, which concerns both the content and the ways of action, originates in rationality, but inasmuch as it implies the actual transcending of the self by itself, it is traceable, in strict appropriateness, to the way of subsisting and to the way of acting which belong to a complete substance of rational nature. In short, it is traceable to personality.[21] Qualities are transcended and the rela-

[21] In contemporary discussions about individual and person some obscurity may have been caused by a tendency to consider personality as the proper cause of features which actually originate in rational nature, more precisely, in rationality as man's specific difference. To be sure, individuality proceeds from the material component of things composite, and personality from what is most formal in man, viz., the rationality of his nature. It remains that rationality and personality are distinct principles of explanation. The former belongs to the constitution of a nature, the latter belongs to the way of subsisting and to the subsequent way of acting that are proper to a nature constituted in its species by rationality. Whether or not we have any use for the word "personalism," only propositions referring in strict appropriateness to personality can

tion of friendship is established on its true basis. As long as it is directed to quantities, friendship remains uncertain: it achieves complete genuineness only when it exists between person and person, regardless of what happens to the qualities of the beloved. Then, the question *why* one loves is best answered—if this can be called an answer—by pointing to what is unique and unutterable about a person. This state of affairs is well described in a celebrated essay of Montaigne. "If I am entreated to say why I loved him, I feel that this cannot be expressed except by answering 'Because it was he, because it was I.' Beyond all my discourse and whatever I can say distinctly about it, I do not know what unexplainable and overwhelming force is instrumental in such a union."[22] In all likelihood Pascal was commenting on Montaigne when he wrote these words: "But if one loves another one because of his beauty, does he love him? No: for smallpox, which kills the beauty without killing the person, will put an end to love. And if one loves me for my judgment, for my memory, does one love me? No, for I can lose these qualities without losing myself. But where is this self, if it is neither in the body, nor in the soul? and how would it be possible to love the body and the soul, except for these qualities, which do not constitute the self, since they are perishable? should one love the substance of the soul of a person abstractly, and regardless of the qualities in it? that

---

be meaningfully considered parts of a personalistic doctrine. If a proposition relative, say, to the rights of man, derives all its truth and power from a relation to the rationality of man's nature, it does not belong to any variety of personalism, but can be held by any philosophy able to recognize the image of God in man.

[22] *Essays*, Bk. I, ch. 27.

cannot be, and that would be unfair. Thus, one never loves any person, but only qualities."[23]

The last sentence will be misunderstood unless it is held to express the sorrowful perplexity of a man who does not see the answer to a question that he has stated with extreme keenness. Pascal knows that the object of genuine love cannot be anything else than the self. Then, perhaps with some bitterness, he turns to the fact that people are liked and loved because of their qualities, which seems to imply that they never are loved genuinely and that they are bound to remain unhappy. Both in terms of natural possibility and in terms of justice, he sees no way out of this fateful state of affairs. Apparently, he is not unaware of the difference between "being an object of love," and "being a ground of love"; on the one hand, he speaks of loving a person *because of* his beauty, *for* his judgment, *for* his memory; on the other hand, he speaks of loving qualities, not persons. To get more out of the distinction between ground and object of love, let us see in what sense friendship can make itself independent of its own grounds. Indeed, the only thing that human love cannot do is to create out of nothing the goodness, the desirability of its object. Divine love alone causes the beloved to be good, independently of any goodness antecedent to love. In order to be an object for the love of a creature, a thing must already be good: in that sense it is true that no one is loved or liked by his fellow men except for his qualities. But, although many of these qualities are subject to destruction—the first example of Pascal is beauty—a human being will never be totally devoid of qualities.

[23] *Pensées,* frag. 323 (New York: Modern Library, 1941), p. 109.

There will always be in him a ground, or a multiplicity of grounds, for disinterested love. Even though a lady has been loved for her beauty, smallpox does not necessarily cause her to be neglected. Under the worst of circumstances, the excellence of human nature, considered in actual existence and in relation to its end, would still be a perfect ground for loving a person without measure. And this excellence of man becomes an infinitely more powerful ground of love when man is considered in the mystery of his supernatural relation to God. Pascal seems to have missed, at least in the present fragment, this ability of love to transcend qualities and be concerned with persons. But without such ability, the other-centered needs which bind men together would be sheer facts of nature and in no way pertain to reason and freedom. Friendship would be impossible. And civic virtue would be impossible.

To sum all up, let us again imagine that the members of a community, in a supreme act of boundless dedication, resolve to will and intend, under all circumstances, the matter of the common good as well as its form. By this resolution the particular capacity is abolished: from now on, it will be up to the common capacity to take care of the most particular business.

As far as the function is concerned, the disappearance of the particular capacity results in a loss of order, and among the forms which make up order those are more directly and seriously damaged which are rational in character. As far as the subject is concerned, the disappearance of the particular capacity entails also a loss of order, and this damage is greater where order is mostly made of historical settlement. If the particularity of the subject alone were impaired, and its ordering power transferred to the function, as in the *Republic* of Plato, whatever is historical in the arrangement of the state would be replaced by a rational disposition, and this would make a great deal of difference, for any impairment of particularity, in the case of the subject, entails a loss of antonomy.

It is the excellence of autonomy which vindicates the particularity of the subject and whatever forms of authority are needed for the preservation of this particularity. Here, familiar contrasts are transcended, authority and autonomy no longer conflict with each other and no longer restrict each other. They cause and guaranty one another. But a rebel cannot perceive the great unity, the great peace which obtains at this very deep level of social reality. Autonomy implies the interiority of the law, a condition which, for human agents at least, is not native, but has to be achieved through arduous progress. Rebels hate the sacrifices that the interiorization of the law requires. It is bad enough for them that the law should exist outside man, and hover around after the fashion of a threat. Autonomy will never lead them to the understanding of authority, for their notion of autonomy is itself a counterfeit.*

* In a slightly different form, Chapter 2 of this book originally appeared in the *Review of Politics,* XXII, no. 2 (April 1960), published by the University of Notre Dame Press, Notre Dame, Indiana. It is reprinted here with the permission of the *Review's* editors.

CHAPTER *3*

The Search for Truth

So far our discussion has been entirely relative to action and practical judgment. We now propose to study the role of authority in the relation of the human mind to theoretical truth. To obtain clear definitions of these two orders, the theoretical and the practical, let us formulate the questions that we strive to answer in each of them. Every practical cognition is designed to answer, directly or indirectly, the questions "What ought we to do?" "What should we have done?" "What shall we do?" The ultimate answer to the practical question is a command, i.e., a judgment so related to action as to constitute its form.[1] Inasmuch as a judgment is meant to be

[1] As recalled at the beginning of most textbooks of logic, proposition (or enunciation, or sentence) is only one form of speech among several. In the case of what we call the ultimate pratical judgment there is *oratio imperativa,* command, not proposition. Yet it is proper to speak of judgment, for the specific component of the act of judging is not the proposition but the *assent* given by the mind to a truth which is one of cognition when the matter of the judgment is a proposition, and one of direction when the matter of the judgment is purely that of a command. It is hardly necessary to remark that the features of the proposition and those of the command may combine and make up a variety of arrangements. The *ultimate* practical judgment is a sheer command. But many practical judgments, on diverse levels of abstraction and generality, command actions in a variety of ways without ceasing to be assents to *propositions*. These mixed types, resulting from

the form of an action, truth consists in conformity to the requirements of sound intention. A decision made under conditions of perfect wisdom may, by reason of contingency, bring about failure. Then it must be granted that a judgment of fact turned out to be false. But the decision itself, as form of human action, was precisely what honesty and wisdom wanted it to be under the circumstances, and this agreement with right intention is the truth proper to the practical judgment.

Just as practical cognition is an answer to the question "What ought we to do?", so theoretical cognition is defined as an answer to the question "What are the things?" By this definition, any judgment whose perfection consists in conformity to a real state of affairs[2] is theoretical. To be sure, theory and judgments of fact are commonly set in opposition, but this opposition itself is best vindicated in the present description. Inasmuch as the purpose of the theoretical mind is to know what things are, explanatory knowledge is the more genuine, and accordingly the more theoretical part of the theoretical order. It is proper to call theory the system in which the perfection of theoretical knowledge, i.e., the explanation of things, is attained or at least striven for. But explanatory knowledge is only a distinguished way of answering the question "What are the things?", and the initial answer

propositions inclined toward action and from incompletely determinate commands, are one of the greatest difficulties of the theory of practical knowledge.

[2] In this proposition "real" must be interpreted (1) as admitting of degrees, for what is real in act is more real than what is real in potency, and (2) as standing for a set which includes non-real states of affairs constructed by the mind after the pattern of real entities; the truth of a judgment relative to beings of reason is just as theoretical as the truth of a judgment relative to real beings.

to the same question, viz., the statement of fact, belongs to the same order. Primarily, theory means contempla- ⟩ tion. Anything can be contemplated: a landscape, a child, an historical event or a transcendental property of being. Although the contemplative operations of the mind are mostly concerned with causes and principles, there is also such a thing as a contemplative and non-practical attitude toward the particular and the fact.[3]

[3] Michael Polanyi [*The Logic of Liberty* (Chicago: University of Chicago Press, 1951), p. 3] gives two examples of disinterested knowledge, one of which concerns the demonstration of the theorem of Fermat and the other the number of molecules which make up the universe. The latter resembles very much the question, "How many pebbles are there in the bed of the river?", the answer to which would not increase in any way the perfection of the theoretical intellect (*Sum. Theol.* i-ii. 14. 3; i. 94. 3). Indeed, the perfection of the theoretical intellect is made of understanding, and essential relations are the only things that can be understood in an unqualified sense. Answering the question, "How many pebbles are there in the bed of the river?" may be of practical relevance; but the answer to this question does not procure the state of excellence proper to the theoretical intellect. Thus let us not identify "theoretical" question and "theoretically-relevant" question. The questions concerning such sheer facts as the number of pebbles in the bed of the river or the number of molecules in the universe are theoretical though, in themselves, devoid of theoretical relevance. We say "in themselves" because the answer to questions of this type often *leads to* the understanding of intelligible relations, in which case questions and answers become theoretically relevant in an indirect manner. As far as the psychology of research is concerned, it is generally imprudent to declare that a question is theoretically irrelevant: who can say that it will not, some day, lead to the understanding of some essential relation? For instance, the extreme scarcity of a certain kind of stone in the bed of a river may lead us to the understanding of laws concerning the chemicals out of which this stone is made. Likewise, if a living species is represented by very few individuals, this fact of scarcity may lead to theoretically-relevant information concerning the circumstances of its reproduction, concerning its relation to physical and chemical environment and to other species, etc.

THE WITNESS

In the study of the theoretical functions of authority let us never lose sight of this fundamental contrast: when an issue is one of action, not of truth, the person in authority has the character of a leader; but when the issue is one of truth, not of action, the person in authority has the character of a witness. Indeed, a witness may also be a leader and, in the capacity of leader, exercise command. But in the mere witness, and universally in the witness as such, authority does not involve, in any sense or degree, the power to give orders and to demand obedience. We would say that an event, for some time considered doubtful, finally has been established by the authority of sound and numerous witnesses. We would go so far as to say that yielding to their testimony is a duty and a matter of honesty. Under many circumstances there is a moral obligation to believe in facts that we did not see and that others have seen; but this obligation does not originate in a command elicited by the witnesses; it originates in a law that these people did not make. Witnesses do not enjoy, in human relations, a position superior to ours. The authority of the mere witness is nothing else than truthfulness as expressed by signs which make it recognizable in varying degrees of assurance.

Authority so understood plays a large part in the cognition of theoretical truth. Among the propositions communicated from mind to mind, both in daily and in scholarly life, only a few can be readily verified by the receiver. If every purchaser insisted on repeating for himself the addition made by the salesman, with or without the help of an adding machine, stores would be bottle-necked at busy hours. In the division of the scientific process each worker, for reasons that are overwhelming without being essential, constantly depends upon the testimony of his fellow workers. There is no essential reason why one and the same man should not be both an experimental and a theoretical physicist. But because our life is short and our versatility limited, every physicist confines his effort to either the theoretical or the experimental field and consents to be a mere believer in the field which is not his. Even within his own field he can see only a few things for himself and has to take the word of others in many cases. Scientific facts, indeed, are essentially renewable, and scientific demonstrations and computations admit of being repeated by indefinitely many persons. The necessity of believing, in science, is merely factual: yet it covers a high ratio of the propositions assented to by any scientific mind.

With regard to historical facts the need to believe takes on a distinct meaning. In the history of the physical world as well as in that of mankind, every fact is unique and unrenewable. True, strict singularity does not always exclude inference according to physical causality, e.g., a footprint sometimes makes it possible to determine both the species of an animal and the date of its passage. But the portion of the human past which can be attained by physical evidence is little in comparison with what can be known only through testimony. Barring the good luck of physical evidence, whoever was not present when and where the event took place has to choose between complete ignorance and dependence upon the authority of witnesses. And this is how all men, including the proudest among the rationalists, the liberals and the anarchists, hold true, with an assurance which admits of degrees but sometimes attains certitude, a great number of propositions, upon the authority of other men.

The notion that assent to a theoretical truth may ever be determined by authority involves a paradox. Let us refer to the method of determination which obtains in the most perfect kind of theoretical knowledge, i.e., demonstration. In the simplest case a theory proposes to connect with each other, by the copula *is,* a subject *S* and a property *P.* I do not yet know if it should be said that *S* is *P;* the synthesis is merely enunciated, and I do not know, as yet, if it conforms to reality. Demonstration is a discursive operation designed to show, through the power of obvious principles, that there exists a relation of conformity between the interconceptual synthesis and the real world, and that the proposition which connects *S* and *P* does in its own way precisely what reality does in a different way. I have understood the demonstration and I have understood that it holds when I have come to perceive that the object designated by *S* would not be what it is—that it would be both identical with itself and different from itself—if it were not united with the object *P.* Then the synthesis "S is P" is no longer merely enunciated; it is asserted. It has received the assent of the mind and by this assent has been promoted from a state of weakness and potency to a state of firmness and actuality. Judgment is entirely formed when the mind, by perceiving the truth of a proposition, i.e., its conformity with the real, assents to this proposition.

A merely probable reasoning inclines the mind toward a conclusion but does not do away with the fear of error. On the contrary, the truth of the demonstrated proposition has been made obvious. Discursive work has dis-

engaged it from darkness with such complete success as
to necessitate assent. Considering that the proper object
of judgment is the relation of truth, let it be said that
whenever assent is totally determined by truth, the object holds an unqualified power of decision. Such victory of objectivity is the perfection of knowledge. *Under
fully normal circumstances the determination of the
theoretical assent involves neither authority nor liberty:
it is an issue settled by objectivity alone.*[4] Because to
know is to be an object, we know poorly and we fail to
know whenever the object undergoes an alteration and
whenever its power is held in check. Theoretical knowledge requires, as the essence of its perfection, an object
disclosed under conditions of absolute purity and independence.[5]

[4] It is hardly necessary to recall that theoretical science admits
of diverse forms of objectivity. Diversity in the forms of objectivity
entails significant differences both in terms of reality and in terms
of necessity. If the subject-matter is logical, a proposition is true
by conformity to an object which is itself logical and, as such,
grounded in the world of reality. If the subject-matter is mathematical, the object to which the true proposition conforms is
always, though in a variety of ways, beside or outside the world of
reality. Further, most contemporary mathematicians have come to
interpret the necessity of mathematical conclusions as postulational, i.e., as ultimately dependent upon premises which, though
reasonably assumed, remain devoid of self-evidence and do not, of
themselves, necessitate the mind.

[5] These conditions do not by any means involve exhaustiveness.
Human knowledge is never exhaustive. In exhaustive knowledge,
the object is, from any conceivable or imaginable point of view,
identical with the thing known, but in man, the most true, the
most thorough, the most exact knowledge never succeeds in con-
ferring the state of object upon more than some aspect of the thing
known. No matter how clearly this aspect is attained there remains
behind it something that may be designated, with equal propriety,
as a transobject or as a mystery and which calls for new acts of

To this ideal of demonstrative knowledge some oppose, as a more exalted conception, what they call the
creative freedom of the mind. True, the progress of
thought commonly uses a variety of constructs. But the
term toward which there is progress is determinate
knowledge, not free construction. The object of determinate knowledge is not necessarily real:[6] beings of
reason crowd the science of mathematics and the mathematical interpretation of nature. They constitute the
object of logic in its entirety. All beings of reason owe
their existence to the activity of the mind, but the only
ones which can be said to be freely created—chimerae,
undines, etc.—belong to literature, not to science. The
scientific beings of reason imply a necessary constitution.
Logical entities are particularly famous for the inflexible
firmness with which they impose their forms upon the
mind. Whether we are concerned with real beings or
beings of reason, and no matter how important the part
played by creative freedom in the phases of approach,
all the processes of theoretical life are terminated by

---

cognition and for *indefinite* progress in an apprehension never
equal to the knowability of the thing. On the position that "to
know is to be an object" see *On The Soul*, 3.5, 430a 14-15, 20; 3.7.
431a1; 3.8. 431b 20-23.

[6] When the object of true knowledge is a being of reason (*ens
rationis*), the proposition that truth consists in the conformity of
judgment to the real does not hold directly. It still holds, however,
indirectly and fundamentally, inasmuch as the case of the real is
primary and retains its primariness under all circumstances. There
are diverse kinds of truths in relation to diverse kinds of objects.
These truths and these objects make up analogical sets where the
role of first analogate is played by the real and the truth of the
judgment in conformity to it. The definition of the first analogate
makes it possible to determine the meaning of the analogical concept in each and every one of its determinations.

acts of knowledge. Now, an act of knowledge never expresses a free choice except insofar as the object remains hidden, in other words, insofar as, for lack of objectivity in act, knowledge suffers an admixture of nonknowledge. Whenever research ends in free construction, the theoretical intellect has undergone a setback. In more precise language, let it be said that such research actually fails to conclude, remains tentative and retains the character of an approach. Setbacks of this kind may be frequent; in intellectual life, as well as in other parts of this world of contingency, successful achievements are few.

Some would argue that in such domains as the mathematical interpretation of nature the constructs of thought are never transcended; the latest step forward would never be anything else than a new or an improved construct. True, inasmuch as the problem, here, is to know nature, research which ends in a construct does not really end, and its scientific character remains qualified. But it should also be remarked that the process which elicits, constructs, and endlessly replaces those that are obsolete by up-to-date ones, leaves behind itself a silently growing treasure of definitively established propositions which, through the adventures of the hypothetical and deductive method, have reached a genuinely scientific condition. Compare the physics of our time with that of the 16th century: although every part of physics contains constructs, none of which is immune to reconsideration, there is at the core of our physics a body of propositions which are given additional assurances by every scientific revolution. Little noise is made about these propositions. Whitehead remarked that, in order to know the deepest beliefs of a philosophical period, attention should turn to the things of which the

philosophers never speak. Likewise, in order to know
what is best established and most genuinely scientific in
physics it may be necessary to inquire into subjects
which, by reason of their being settled in uncontroverted
fashion, lie beneath the level of articulate expression.

The interpretation of scientific knowledge as creative
freedom often expresses the sentiment that the dignity
of the mind is not compatible with the necessary determination of its judgments. A strong feeling for this dignity would oppose the theory which places the perfection
of knowledge in the victory of a pure and untouched
object. This involves a misunderstanding made easy by
the use of inadequate language. In order to express the
power of the subject in obvious knowledge, many would
say that the mind is *forced* or constrained to assent: these
words convey pictures of violence which distort the
whole situation. When the mind is confronted by an obvious proposition, accompanied by all the conditions of
its obviousness, it can neither utter an assent contrary to
truth nor withhold its assent and remain silent. The
only thing that can be done by act of will is to remove
attention. I may, at will, think of the principle of causality, or of the law of real distinction between essence and
existence or think of none of these propositions; but I
cannot think of an immediately evident proposition with
a clear understanding of its terms, or think of a demonstrated proposition under the power of the demonstration, and judge that these propositions are untrue, or
withhold my judgment. There is no constraint in the
necessity that obvious truth brings about in the mind,
for constraints is a necessity from without and a violence
done to the spontaneity of the subject. When the intellect assents to obvious truth, it acts according to what is
most intimate in its own nature. *The victory of objectiv-*

ity is also a victory of intellectual vitality. There is nothing more profound in the life of the intellect than our eagerness to know, without tepidity and without fear, under conditions of a certitude totally determined by the power of truth.

To explain the character of this determination, let us recall that there are two kinds of passivity. In the material or physical universe, "to undergo," "to be acted upon" always designates an event in which the subject acted upon loses some determination, for which another determination, issued from an external agent, is substituted. The passions of material things are heteronomic, inasmuch as the law embodied in them is not that of the patient, but that of the agent. It is the privilege of the soul to receive forms and perfections without undergoing concomitant losses. A purely advantageous passion is autonomic inasmuch as what is received is the achievement of the subject, its actuation, its accomplishment, according to its own law and under the influence of a friendly principle.[7] The law of the mind resembles the law of the object in the way in which potential and actual being resemble each other. The intellect is, in potency, and desires to be, in act, what the object actually is. By receiving the determining influence of the object, by becoming the object, determinately, exactly, in precise coincidence, it is, in a very deep sense, changed into itself.[8]

Again, the state of perfection in which the intellect

[7] *On the Soul,* 2.5. 417b2.

[8] For this reason Aristotle *(On The Soul,* 2.5. 417b 5-8) denies that the knower is changed or altered in any ordinary sense; rather there takes place a development into his true self. Objective knowledge, far from being an alienation (alteration) of the knower from his true self, is the only remedy (soteria, 417b2) for the alienation which is ignorance, error, doubt. Cf. 418 a 1-5.

is totally determined by the object is rare. All men enjoying the normal use of reason perceive, in very unequal degrees of intensity, the obviousness of the first principles and of the general propositions pertaining to immediate experience. People trained in the sciences understand some immediate propositions whose meaning is not accessible to ordinary men. With regard to demonstrated propositions it should be noticed (1) that absolutely rigorous demonstrations, the only ones which bring about obviousness and the necessary determination of the mind by the object are few and (2) that under the best circumstances the number of demonstrations actually understood by a person is very small. Such is the condition of the human mind: obviousness is strictly required for its normal life, yet it is unobtainable in most cases. For lack of obviousness we often have to give up certainty, to content ourselves with opinions, to utter assents weakened by the fear of error. In many cases this fear is not removed by the testimony of persons who claim to have observed a fact or perceived the obviousness of a demonstration. Yet it also happens that a testimony is held entirely trustworthy; then we paradoxically give a firm assent to a truth which remains obscure and incapable of a necessitating action upon the mind. Objectivity is held in check by obscurity. An assent which is firm without being necessary cannot be anything else than voluntary. It owes its ultimate determination, its certitude, to an act of confidence. By deciding to trust the witness held reliable, we dismiss the fear of error and bring about a state of affairs unattainable by cognitive process alone. The foundation of confidence, i.e., the authority of the witness, plays a part which under better circumstances would pertain to the object. Authority is

used as a substitute for objectivity, it exercises a function
which properly belongs to the object but actually cannot be exercised by it. Because of a defect in the relation
between mind and object, the intervention of authority
makes sense. With regard to the determination of the
theoretical judgment, the function of authority is substitutional. Whenever there is a question of knowing
what the things are, and of determining whether or not
a proposition conforms to reality, the appeal to authority
is justified only by a defective situation, viz., by the situation of an intellect that is denied clarity.

It is easy to indulge in rhetorical statements about the
freedom of the mind, and it looks chivalrous to side with
"pure truth" against authority.[9] But to keep living and
thinking, we must, at the next instant, take the word of
witnesses who have seen things that we do not see, that
we have not seen, and in many cases, that we do not expect ever to see. The simple consideration that the role
of authority in theoretical matters is entirely substitutional makes it easy to understand both how docility to
reliable witnesses proceeds from the love of truth, and
how the love of truth stirs an indefatigable eagerness for
a cognition in which authority no longer plays any part.
If truth is loved, the main thing is to know it. If truth
cannot be known obviously, it is good to know it by way

[9] Let attention be called to an accident often observed in
academic life both among young people and among their elders.
Those who, as a result of rebelliousness, poor judgment or bad
luck fail to identify the dependable witnesses are the most eager
to accept prejudices and clichés. When the failure to receive the
proper guidance is accompanied by boasting about "critical-mind-
edness," prejudices, clichés and gossip are readily accepted. Understandably, when the higher ways of social causality fail to provide
the needed guidance, we get a low class indoctrination marked by
what is least vital and least intelligent in social life.

of belief. Likewise, when it is impossible to live with a friend, we still say that we remain close to him. No one would wish to forget his friend as soon as it becomes impossible to live in his company. A mere union in thought and affection is an unsatisfactory substitute for common life and common action; yet it is, by all means, preferable to the complete separation that oblivion would constitute. Friendship itself demands and maintains such a union, although it steadily refuses to be satisfied with it, and love for truth takes us into the darkness of belief when truth cannot be known in clarity. Only those who do not love truth would prefer ignorance to belief, since belief is able to preserve, no matter how imperfectly, the union of the mind with truth. But nothing, save indifference to truth, can prevent us from experiencing, in belief, an uncompromising desire for vision.

THE TEACHER

Reluctance to believe is commonly silent in the domain of the unrenewable events which make up history. Provided that the historical event does not directly threaten our conception of life—as may happen in the case of a miracle, in that of a crime committed by our friends, or of a good action done by our enemies—two obvious considerations render belief easily acceptable. For one thing, we generally have no choice, and life, as well as thought, would soon become impossible if every narrative were held dubious. Moreover, the most rebellious mind feels no aversion to the authority of a witness who does not claim, on any ground, a right to be obeyed.

When truth is such as to admit of being verified by an unlimited multitude of persons, it is entirely normal that our attitude toward witnesses should be substantially different. However, authorities are treated without hostility so long as things do not involve a social relation of superior to inferior. Why should not the theoretical physicist be willing to receive facts from a laboratory worker? The experimental physicist is not empowered by society to give the theorist orders, and there is no danger that an argument derived from social hierarchy should ever be used to strengthen the authority of a colleague whose function is to observe physical facts.

The relation of teacher to pupil constitutes an altogether different situation. Within the limits of the tasks over which he presides, the teacher has the power to issue orders and to make sure that they are carried out. He directs the student to do some readings and to make some observations, to memorize some formulas and texts, to write reports and essays, and to take examinations at definite times. Indeed, this gentleman, who is endowed with a right to obedience in external acts connected with the work of learning, demands that the student should trust him in theoretical matters, in other words, should hold some propositions true precisely because the teacher certifies that they are such. But here trouble arises and the classroom splits into three groups: those who are perfectly submissive because their only interest is to get a credit, those who are said to have powerfully critical minds, and those described as intelligently teachable. The first group does not really belong to theoretical life. The relevant comparison is between the latter two; let it be said that teachable students learn faster and better, provided the teacher is good.

For the sake of clarity we shall consider the case of a
scientific matter. The laws of knowledge demand that
the obviousness of the object be the sufficient cause of
the assent. But in order to perceive the obviousness of
difficult demonstrations one needs to have already a good
scientific training. The development of every science
student comprises a phase of apprenticeship in which
particularly easy demonstrations alone are understood.
What will happen, during this period of decisive significance, to the many and important truths so hard to
demonstrate that their obvious necessity cannot be perceived at once?[10] Two attitudes are possible: either we
shall withhold our judgment, or we shall trust the
teacher and consent that his authority should, for a while,
play the part of an obviousness not readily accessible.
"Critical" minds prefer the withholding of judgment
and vindicate it through never ending objections. They
are not satisfied unless they silence the teacher and stop
the work of teaching. To be sure, there are many cases
in which the process of acquiring knowledge needs, in
order to go on, the firm basis of a definite assent. If such
assent, for lack of a sufficient background, cannot assume
the character of scientific cognition, it must assume that
of belief; otherwise the student is no longer learning.
Teachable minds have the privilege of understanding
that a provisional belief often is the best, or the strictly
indispensable way, to science.[11] Of course, the belief

10 Let it be recalled that obviousness, philosophically understood, is an objective property and does not imply the readiness of
any knower to grasp it at once.

11 The words of Aristotle, "the one who is in the process of learning must believe" (*On Soph. Refutations*, 2. 165 b3) were often
interpreted as referring to this need for confidence and willingness
to take the word of a teacher. *Oportet addiscentem credere* is the

used by the beginner as a means to understanding admits of degrees. In some cases, which may be very important, the assent given on the teacher's authority is
entirely firm and excludes the fear of error, but in most
cases it has no more weight than a mere opinion, at all
times subject to reconsideration. As for the teacher
whose ambition is to be believed permanently, he is
guilty of extreme dishonesty, no matter how true his
propositions. In spite of appearances which soon no
longer deceive anyone, he is not teaching scientific truth,
since he is not eager to replace, in the minds intrusted
to his attention, belief by science. To prove that he is
reliable, a teacher must convince his pupils that they
never should use his reliability as an excuse to spare
themselves the hardships of intelligent apprehension.

---

proverbial expression of the need for a phase of belief at a time
when science is not yet possible. This could have been meant by
Aristotle, but does not seem to be what he actually means in this
particular passage. In Greek and in several other languages, the
verb expressing the act of believing (Greek, *pisteúein*), as distinct
from the act of clear cognition, also can express the act of assent-
ing firmly, whether assent takes place by way of trust in a witness
or by way of clear determination. In the present passage, *pisteúein*
seems to have this broader meaning. In opposition to the dialecti-
cian, who is satisfied with verisimilitude and the weak assent of
opinion, the one who is in the process of learning *tòn manthán-
onta*), i.e., of acquiring *science,* is concerned with firm assent. The
process of learning will not be terminated until the firm assent of
scientific knowledge has replaced the opinion that a merely dialectical process can impart.

See the note of Edward Post, *Aristotle on Fallacies, or The
Sophistici Elenchi* (London: 1866), text p. 4, note 2 in Appendix,
pp. 102-103. It is thus a striking fact that something not altogether
unlike the "credo ut intelligam" doctrine of St. Augustine and St.
Anselm is to be found in Aristotle on a natural level, as a condition of the learning situation. Cf. St. Thomas Aquinas, *Exposition of Boethius on The Trinity,* 3.1, translated by V. J. Bourke in
The Pocket Aquinas (New York: 1960), pp. 288-289.

The organization of a school requires a sharp division between students and teachers. It postulates, accordingly, that a time comes when the scientific man ceases to be a student, ceases to be a beginner, ceases to be a scientific mind in the process of training, and ceases to need the direction of a teacher. Save from an administrative standpoint, this postulation is nonsense. A learned professor exercises true mastery over but a part of the demonstrations which make up his field; for all the rest, he is in the condition of a student and must consent to believe not only in order not to be frequently interrupted in his teaching by the gaps of his demonstrative system, but also in order to give himself a chance to achieve progress in understanding. He is no longer placed under the orders of an elder commissioned by society to direct his research and to give him grades. Yet the men whom he quotes are not mere witnesses: they often are authentic teachers who, whether alive or dead, carry out pedagogical tasks sanctioned by society. Here social influence supports the authority of Descartes and Kant, elsewhere that of Aristotle and St. Thomas, elsewhere that of Hume and Mill, elsewhere that of Karl Marx. Until the beginning of the 19th century, Hippocrates was commissioned by all Western societies to teach medicine to physicians. For more than one century the same societies commissioned Newton to teach physics to physicists. Closer to us, several generations of biologists have been subjected to the teaching authority of the theorists of evolution. In spite of common pronouncement against "the method of authority" modern societies are very anxious to designate the teachers that students and professors will have to listen to. These teachers are more numerous than in the past, and they change more often.

The intervention of society in intellectual life aroused much aversion through misuse and failure. It has often protected error. Yet, to realize that it is a thing normal and necessary, it suffices to consider the insuperable difficulties that the choice of a guide would involve if society remained silent. Since no scholar achieves any skill in any domain without having gone through a phase of apprenticeship and belief, the choice of a guide takes place at a time when the mind is still unable to estimate the value of theories and systems. The young man does not know where to go and his parents would not be less embarrassed if society did not tell them, through the voice of persons whose dependability it certifies, that in anatomy Grant is better than Aristotle and that in philosophy Plato is better than Herbert Spencer. But every scholar remains a student. Throughout his life he is confronted with the necessity of trusting those who, on such and such a subject, know more than he does: until the last day of his research, his docility needs to be directed and stimulated.

Consider now by what methods society assigns teachers to eager minds. In the fields of knowledge where truth is relatively easy to communicate and relatively easy to recognize, the influence of society is mostly exercised by way of spontaneous relations. Thus, as far as positive sciences are concerned, the duty to designate teachers belongs to the *society of the persons trained in the positive sciences:* it is neither a state nor a church, and it is not a society in the full sense of this term. The agreement of the minds, as expressed in the activities of learned groups and in scientific publications, constitutes the best method of direction, in fields where truth is very likely to prevail by its own power and by the power of its consequences. But, in such domains as theoretical philosophy and ethics, agreement is unlikely to extend factually beyond a group of kindred minds. Neither the catalogues of the publishing companies, nor the journals read by the specialists, nor the learned academies will help the beginner puzzled by the multiplicity of philosophic schools and their never-ending conflicts. No spontaneous operation of intellectual relations protects the young philosopher against the risk of delivering his soul to error by choosing his teachers infelicitously. This major difficulty will be considered in the following discussion on intellectual freedom.

THE FREEDOM OF THE INTELLECT

The expression "freedom of the intellect," which admits of several meanings, sometimes designates nothing else than the defeat of such forces of error and ignorance as passions and prejudices, blind traditions and unreasonable fashions, the imperialism of schools and the arbitrary dogmatism of their programs, the prestige of national groups, the imposture of false witnesses, insincerity in all its descriptions and, above all, the tough selfishness of the intellectual ego by reason of which systems, instead of bringing truth into the mind, act as screens between the mind and the truth. If the question is to achieve all this and nothing else, whoever loves truth cherishes with the same heart the freedom of the intellect, and no one is interested in intellectual freedom unless he loves truth. So understood, intellectual free-

dom has the character of a cause, most precious and
always in danger. It transcends the programs of all
schools of thought and parties. It has no particular connection with the philosophical and historical entity
known under the name of liberalism. In spite of its
many adversaries, it remains a universally human cause
and cannot constitute the distinctive purpose of any
system or movement.

Turning to the notion of intellectual freedom such
as it is conceived in liberalism, let us try to determine
what is distinctively liberal about it. The answer would
be relatively simple if it were possible to say that of all
interpretations of intellectual freedom, only one belongs properly to liberalism. But this is not the case. In
the historical reality of the liberal movements, the freedom of the intellect is the subject of several interpretations, all of which deserve, on diverse grounds and in
diverse degrees, to be considered typical expressions of
liberal thought. Our exposition of these interpretations
will begin with the most radical, which is also the least
frequently expressed, and end with the most constant,
which is also the least radical.

*

*   *

The structure of the mind can be described in terms
of a polar opposition. Judgments possessed of immediate
or demonstrative obviousness make up the *pole of rational determination,* and judgments relative to particular goods make up the *pole of practical indifference.*
It is easy to imagine what reductions to unity the philosophers will be tempted to effect. Everything would be
incomparably simpler and our vision of human life
would be rid of much mystery—though perhaps at the

cost of much absurdity—if it were possible to suppress
one of the two centers of attraction and to place all
judgments in the area defined by the remaining center.
Since necessity is really and logically anterior to freedom, reduction to the system of rational determination
was to be attempted first. Rationalistic determinism had
been in existence for many centuries when the opposite
attempt was favored by unprecedented developments,
pertaining mostly to the moral and political order. Beginning with Charles Renouvier (1815-1903) the dialogue of the philosophers comprises a character whose
role is to extend systematically the domain of voluntary
assent. This character is cautious and often noncom-
mittal; most of the time he operates silently. It is generally hard to know what significance he attributes to
his own pronouncements. Yet it is clear that at the logical limit of his undertakings there no longer is such a
thing as necessitating obviousness: even the first principles have become objects of free belief. The pole of rational determination and its field of attraction have
disappeared.

It cannot be said that this most radical interpretation
of intellectual freedom belongs to the essence of liberalism. To be sure, a true liberal may confess that the principle of noncontradiction does not in any way depend
upon the dispositions of our freedom. Only a few extremists openly hold the theory of a free adherence to
the first principles. Yet the influence of this theory has
not been negligible. The paradoxes of the extremists
often convey thoughts which are present and active, perhaps subconsciously, in the minds of the moderates.
Though professed by few persons, the theory of a free
domination over obviousness itself has been haunting

the liberal movement after the fashion of a ghost, hidden most of the time and skilled at concealing his identity, but always ready to lead the liberal conscience into subtle temptations.[12]

[12] The trend described here, which originated in moral and social attitudes, often combined its energy with that of a trend altogether relative to epistemological issues. Ever since the time of the Greek geometricians the axioms of mathematics had been held to constitute the clearest and most unmistakable examples of rational necessity. Over a period of many centuries, mathematical education was, by general assent, in charge of developing and maintaining, in the minds of men, a sense for those necessities that are not of factual but of essential and intelligible character. Now, in the last generations, a thorough reconsideration of mathematical premises has taken place. It has been brought forth that propositions which play the role of premises in one system may be conclusions in another system; the term axiom, which used to convey the inflexible necessity and absolute primacy of the self-evident propositions, has come to be taken as a mere synonym of postulate. It is hardly possible to exaggerate the importance of this reinterpretation of mathematics in modern culture. Indeed, the grounds on which a system of postulates is *chosen* often remain obscure. It is reasonable to suppose that the emphasis on the postulational character of mathematical premises is still due, at least in part, to a reaction against old misconceptions concerning the relations between mathematical necessity and the necessity proper to the things of the real world. From the point of view of the history of culture, what is decisive is that the idea of a *choice* among principles, of a human initiative in matters of first premises, of a human *control* over primary determinations, is active precisely in the area which, for so many centuries, has been reputed to supply the ideal pattern of determination by objective evidence. (James R. Newman in *Introduction* to W. K. Clifford, *The Common Sense of the Exact Sciences*, p. xlii.) Clear statements of the case are extremely rare; but it is easy to detect, in the common discussion of the most important subjects, the underlying theory that, since the first premises of mathematics from being axioms have become postulates, there can be no domain of thought where principles escape the condition of mere assumptions selected by the human mind with some degree of arbitrariness.

Another interpretation of intellectual freedom connects liberalism with agnosticism. Indeed, the first great synthesis of agnostic thought was built, under the name of positive philosophy, by an adversary of most liberal ideas. Paradoxically, many liberal thinkers, whether missing or ignoring the deep intention of Auguste Comte (1798-1857) held that the men of their own spirit were greatly indebted to the founder of positivism. What interested them in Auguste Comte was not the high priest of a distinctly ridiculous religion, narrowly dogmatic and big with a threat of clerical power; neither was it the political heir to Joseph de Maistre and de Bonald, eager to end revolutionary criticism and to establish a definitive state of affairs; nor was it the legislator of scientific thought, who set limits to the audacity of laboratory men as well as to that of theorists, and who blamed with the same heart hypotheses of structure and microscopic investigations. It was the serene assurance, pervading like a harmony, with which Auguste Comte had proclaimed the end of the absolute. To this disquieting theocratist, liberalism was grateful for having emancipated man from the transcendent dogmas of theology and metaphysics. The mind had simultaneously won its freedom and found the ways of its progress.

Agnostic liberalism does not deny that objects can determine, in unique and necessary fashion, the assent of the human mind. But it holds that this property belongs only to observable relations, and to the logical principles which govern the construction of the sciences. Thus, the universe of knowledge is divided into two systems: that of experience organized by logic—let it be called *the positive system*—and that of the proposi-

tions which do not admit of experimental verification
—let it be called *the transcendent system*. Within the
positive system it is granted, and sometimes affirmed
with fanatic dogmatism, that the mind enjoys no choice.
But any assent to transcendent propositions is treated
with diffidence, as if it were expressive of intellectual
debasement. In the willingness to be ruled by the absolute, many positivists saw the ultimate cause of every
servitude. All this looks wonderfully clear as long as no
one remarks that the actual life of the intellect, within
the positive system itself, implies assent to some transcendent propositions, and that the separation proclaimed
with such complete assurance by the agnostic negation
has never been actually observed in any work of
thought.[13]

Great difficulties are felt as soon as there is a question
of going beyond cheap generalities and of defining with
any accuracy the content of the two systems. The transcendent system comprises all propositions relative to
the divine mysteries and the mysterious history of the
relations between God and man. It comprises propositions relative to metaphysical objects, such as the first
cause of the world and its last end. Consistency would

[13] Emile Meyerson has convincingly established that the "products of scientific thought," in other words, the things that the
scientific mind actually has brought about in its effort to create a
scientific interpretation of the universe, do not agree on any point
with the program set by early positivism. His famous investigations
(*Identity and Reality, On Explanation in the Sciences*, etc.) are
limited to the domains of mathematical and physical sciences.
Similar investigations in the moral and social fields would easily
show that here also the "products of scientific thought" express
thorough disregard for the restrictions that positivism holds to be
indispensable conditions of scientific research.

require that it comprise also the great epistemological problems, e.g., the relation of universal ideas to reality and the significance of scientific theories—but then science would prove impossible. It should also comprise the supreme principles of morality, viz., views relative to human destiny, to the meaning of human life, to genuine happiness, to the origin of obligation, etc.— but then would ethics still be possible?

The positive system comprises experimental sciences such as physics, chemistry and biology; mathematics and a minium of logic; the so-called observational sciences —geography, ethnology, anthropology, sociology—; such techniques as industrial mechanics, medicine, psychiatry; positive law; practical ethics, i.e., the rules of behavior recommended both by the moralists in repute and by the people commonly held honest. With a not too exacting mind, with no taste for intellectual adventures, no interest in greatness and no sense for God, a man may remain all his life within the positive system and feel perfectly satisfied.

The association of liberalism with agnostic attitudes is common. However, it would be arbitrary to say that it belongs to the essence of liberalism. In fact, many deists and some ardent believers are among the most typical representatives of liberal psychology. Like the idea of a free adherence to first principles, the agnostic attitude is for liberalism no more than a disquieting connection. However, between these two interpretations of intellectual freedom, there is a difference of great historical significance: because it is less radical and less paradoxical, the second does not need to wear a mask. Of the two familiar personages that haunt the liberal conscience, one generally works secretly and the other openly. Both play important roles, but neither can be identified with the liberal concept of intellectual freedom.

*

*   *

The essence of liberalism, as far as intellectual freedom is concerned, must be defined in relation to the sociology of truth. The contrast between the positive and the transcendent systems is provocative in spite of its obscurities: let it be kept in mind. Everyone holds, without taking the trouble of thinking of it explicitly, that society has the right and the duty to take stands on many issues belonging to the positive system. No social life is possible without rules of positive law promulgated by society and guarantied by sanctions that no one can escape. No society would be possible without a code of practical ethics concerning human life, marriage and family, contracts, property and honor. No society is possible, in modern times at least, without the embodiment in positive law of many scientific and technical conclusions—as in the control of foods and drugs, and in the prevention of infectious diseases or accidents. All this is clear, and disagreements concern only particular cases. It may be argued, for instance, that such and such an inheritance law proceeds from an unsound notion of property, but no one would argue that society has no right to have ideas about property. The efficacy of a vaccination and the desirability of making it mandatory may be questioned; but no one questions the right of society to have ideas in matters of public health. On the contrary, society is commonly denied the right to have ideas in transcendent matters. It is commonly denied the right to take stands on metaphysical issues and on issues pertaining to the ultimate vindication of legal and ethical rules. The transcendent system is held to be the domain of private conscience and of the spiritual power, if there be such a thing. Let society inflict punishment in case of theft or murder; but the principles which vindicate ultimately the prohibition of theft and murder are the concern of my conscience and yours—and of our church, if we please to recognize any. Whether these principles are firm or illusory, whether they effectively guaranty or badly jeopardize the code of practical morality without which no social life is possible, is none of society's business. According to your inclination and your lights, you will adopt, as final vindication of the prohibition of crimes and felonies, the commands of a revealed religion or the precepts of an irreligious rationalism, the inspirations of sentiment or the calculations of self-interest, the desire to be happy with God or the determination to be happy in your own way, the absoluteness of duty or the absoluteness of the supreme good, the requirements of an aesthetic harmony or those of a biological equilibrium; you may also, if you are a pure empiricist, refrain from inquiring into the principles of your actions. All these questions pertain to individual conscience. Society has nothing to say about them, it practices agnosticism without professing it; to profess it would already imply a stand on a transcendent issue.

By identifying this "sociological agnosticism," we think that we have reached what is constant, necessary and distinguishing in the liberal claim for freedom of thought. Whoever holds that society must refrain from any act relative to transcendent truth, and that the search for such truth must be neither directed nor helped in any way by society, is a liberal. And whoever holds that society normally should be concerned with transcendent truths, or some of them, has rejected the liberal notion of intellectual freedom; at least he has decided to keep its dynamism under control.[14]

A man who professes agnosticism cannot help objecting to society's taking stands on questions which according to his philosophy cannot be answered. What is remarkable is that many minds by no means inclined toward agnostic attitudes, nay, provided with firm convictions in religion, in ethics, even in metaphysics, hold that society should never say or do anything on behalf of their most cherished beliefs. Further, it often happens that the same persons interpret sociological agnosticism not as a prudential disposition made necessary by the particularities of a spiritually divided society, but as a philosophy which would still hold under circumstances of spiritual unity.[15]

[14] It is hardly necessary to remark that in the concrete history of ideologies adherence to the liberal principle admits of many degrees. Some great liberal tradtions, viz., those which still prevail in Anglo-Saxon countries, do not forbid the agents of the temporal power to take stands on some metaphysical and religious issues. Atheistic propaganda and the most destructive ethical theories are freely expressed in Great Britain and in the United States; but British and American liberals, with the possible exception of a few fanatics, do not object to the Prime Minister's and the President's recommending, in public speeches and by public acts, prayer and the reading of the Holy Scripture. In most Latin countries on the contrary, the liberal tradition hardly allows that God be mentioned in a public speech. If a statesman in these countries happened to recommend the reading of the Gospel, even believers would feel that he is minding someone else's business.

[15] The following discussion will be principally concerned with those transcendent truths which do not claim any supernatural character, and the word society will stand for civil society. But what holds for civil society often admits of application to other societies, and the disposition which forbids civil society to have ideas in transcendent matters may also determine opposition to organized religion, to all forms of community worship and generally recommend individualistic methods whenever transcendent subjects are involved.

The arguments of sociological agnosticism can be summed up as follows: in order not to inflict any violence upon minds and consciences—the worst kind of violence, indeed—a society should never assert any proposition that is not commonly accepted by its members. The application of this rule causes no particular difficulty in the case of societies which are joined voluntarily and which anyone can leave at will. If you hold that the dogmas professed by spiritualistic groups are a challenge to common sense, keep away from these groups. But everyone involuntarily becomes a member of the state, and from the state no one can secede. The problem of the indispensable harmony between the beliefs of society and those of its members cannot be solved, in the case of the state, by the spontaneous operation of intellectual affinities. The only way to solve it is to reduce the intellectual content of public life to a minimum of propositions so chosen that no normal person can disagree. At this point the distinction between the transcendent and the positive systems plays a significant part, independently of any agnostic presupposition. In fact, positive truths, or at least those of them which directly concern the welfare of temporal society, are commonly accepted by normal persons. Thus, such a general fact as the communicability of infectious germs is hardly questioned by anybody. Only a few rebels object to the basic rules of positive law. And most precepts of daily ethics are acknowledged almost unanimously.

The social destiny of transcendent problems is altogether different. Even if one holds that they admit of definite solutions, it must be granted that in many cases they fail to win the assent of minds. When specialists in these questions meet, they can hardly talk to each other for lack of agreement on definitions and principles. One

affirms that God exists and that he can prove His existence; another says that we shall never know whether or
not there exists a God; another holds that such questions
cannot be decided except by revelation; another, that
the question of the existence of God has merely a pragmatic sense; and still another, that it has no sense at all.
How could the great number of men be expected to reach
unanimity where experts are so far from being unanimous?[16] And yet it is necessary to keep unsegregated, in
the society to which everyone belongs by right of birth
and from which no one can secede, these theists and these
atheists, these believers in theoretical truth and these
pragmatists, these utilitarians, these Kantists, these hed-
onists, these evolutionists, these traditionalists, all these
intellectual species which can stand some sort of unity
when there is a question of positive issues, but prove re-
fractory to any discipline when transcendent issues
are in question. To give any of these species a privilege is to do violence to all the others. For lack of a
common assent, the only possible policy is one of ab-
stention.

In order to clarify the meaning of this argumentation
it is necessary to consider the general problem of the
communication of truth. Some truths are incommunicable by nature; thus, I shall never succeed in making
you know exactly what I mean when I say that the smell
of a damp underwood revives in me, in confused and
moving fashion, such and such experiences of my childhood. Some incommunicable truths are very important,
but whatever their nature and their worth, it is plain

---

[16] We intend to leave entirely out of the discussion the question
of a possible guilt involved in the failure to find the truth about
some transcendent issues. The reader will notice that leaving a
question out is not the same as holding it unsettled in all respects.

that they cannot be included in the collective beliefs of a society.[17]

The obscurity of the problem results from a discrepancy between *de jure* and *de facto* possibilities within the system of communicable truths. Every demonstrable proposition is, *de jure*, communicable without limits. But it often happens that the understanding of a fully demonstrated proposition or even that of an immediately obvious one,[18] requires conditions which are not commonly satisfied in any society. *De jure*, some propositions of metaphysics and ethics are no less communicable than any theorem of geometry or law of biology. But whereas the conditions required for the understanding of mathematics and biology seem to be well assured by our schools and other learned organizations, the conditions necessary to understand the most fundamental theories of metaphysics have never been commonly satisfied in any society. At philosophical conventions deaf men make speeches for other deaf men, and blind men play pantomimes for other blind men, and this will never prove anything against the intrinsic communicability of philosophic truth. Such facts prove nothing else than the reality of contingency and its ability to bring about the

[17] We are speaking here of propositions relative to real situations. As recalled in the first chapter, a proposition concerning what ought to be done by a community may, in spite of contingency, demand the assent of all. The ground of common assent, which is not supplied by rational communicability, may be supplied by affective communion.

[18] I refer to the difficulties involved in the formulation of the first principles. Every sane man grasps the principle of causality and applies it many times a day. But phrasing this principle is an immensely difficult task, which will never be accomplished in such conditions of finality as to exclude further improvement through new discussion.

broadest discrepancies between the life of the mind such
as it would be, if nothing interfered with the necessity
of objective laws, and the real life of our minds, where
factors of disturbance are powerful.

As positive science becomes more aware of its social
destiny, it evidences greater determination to cut down
the discrepancy between *de jure* and *de facto* communicability—as far, at least, as the experts are concerned.
Enrico Fermi used to say that the physicist needs to express himself in "sharp statements," and is inclined to
keep away from areas where such a mode of expression
is impossible. A sharp statement is one which, though
possibly inaccessible to unprepared minds, can be communicated by one expert to another in such a way that
the latter soon is ready to determine whether he agrees
or not, or at least soon knows what he should do in order
to ascertain his own stand on the subject. In the selection of its topics, in the determination of its standpoints,
positive science often resorts to costly exclusions that
philosophers are tempted to deem arbitrary. For instance,
the method which ignores, as far as possible, the qualita-
tive aspect of things and substitutes a system of measur-
able data for the more complex world of our experience,
is motivated, to a large extent, by the privilege of propositions that anyone can easily verify provided he submits
to a code of clearly defined and relatively simple op-
erational rules. The philosopher has no right and no inclination to practice such exclusions and must resign
himself never to win unanimity, no matter how rigorous
his demonstrations, except within small groups of kindred minds. As far as communicability is concerned, the
difference between positive science and philosophy, and
more generally between positive and transcendent truth,

should be expressed in terms of tendencies. Positive science systematically seeks *de facto* communicability among persons concerned. But the exclusions necessarily entailed by such a systematic search are strictly forbidden to philosophers. The law of philosophic thinking is altogether concerned with the objective significance of issues and cannot tolerate a tendency to make sacrifices for the sake of factual communicability.

When temporal society takes a stand on a positive proposition, it is—except for possible accidents and abuses—an easily communicable one. Little risk is involved. Opposition, if there is any, will soon be defeated by the felicitous consequences of the principle newly introduced into social life. But when society takes a stand on a truth whose communication involves great difficulties, it accepts all the hardships and all the risks of a struggle which is likely never to end.

At this point, attention should be called to the historical association of liberal doctrines with the ways of knowledge which became predominant in modern times. Positive science, by bringing about constantly repeated evidence of the conquering power of truth, has filled minds with patterns highly favorable to liberal expectations. The telescope of Galileo sufficed to destroy stubborn errors concerning celestial bodies. A few experiments conducted with rigor transformed into scientific propositions, soon accepted by all, the hypotheses of Pasteur concerning the role of micro-organisms in diseases. The history of the sciences, at least since the Renaissance, fully vindicates an optimistic vision of the conflict between truth and error in the positive system. It is very tempting to extend this vision to all orders of human knowledge without asking whether the factors

which, in positive science and technique, determine the
success of truth, work also, and with the same regularity,
in transcendent matters. Justice Holmes summed up the
liberal tradition when he declared that "The best test
of truth is the power of the thought to get itself accepted
in the competition of the market." The preceding remarks on *de facto* communicability raise the question of
whether this celebrated statement is of general significance, or holds only in a distinguished domain, viz., in
the domain where the success of truth is favored by the
firm communicability of proof.

TRUTH AND COMMUNITY

The problem under discussion would be less difficult
if we first succeeded in formulating the general conditions required for the *spontaneous production of order*.
In some cases, a set of random events brings about results that can be predicted with constant success. If a die
is cast according to the rules of the game, any particular
face will turn up about one time out of every six. Calling
"favorable case" the turning up of a selected face, let it
be said (1) that there will be a discrepancy between the
factual ratio of favorable cases to the total number of
trials and the *a priori* formula of probability 1/6; (2)
that, as the series of trials goes on, this discrepancy increases indefinitely in absolute value; and (3) that it de-
creases indefinitely in relative value. Each individual
result is unpredictable. Indeed, without disorderliness
on the part of the individual events, no statistical order
would emerge: that is why the player shakes the die in
the cup and acts absentmindedly. The fact that order is
in some way produced by disorder is unquestioned. The
whole controversy is about the cause of this paradoxical

happening. Referring to Aristotle's analysis of chance[19] (*automaton*), it is quite appropriate to say that this production of order is spontaneous, or automatic. The words "spontaneous," "spontaneity," are used by several translators for the word *automaton,* whereby Aristotle designates an end-like event which actually happened without having been intended either by nature or by reason.[20] In spontaneity so understood, *things take care of themselves,*[21] and a desirable result is attained just by allowing a plurality of causes to act independently of any plan. An example would be the way truth takes care of itself in the competition of the market, according to Justice Holmes.

Aristotle's analysis deals with an individual event which, in spite of its end-likeness, is easily distinguished from intended events. The end-like event which happens automatically has no ground in any essential unity: accordingly, it is a rare occurrence.[22] A desperate person may jump out of the window precisely at the time when a truck loaded with mattresses passes by. The landing is smooth, but this should not be expected to happen twice.

[19] *Ph.* 2. 4-6.

[20] When he needs to be specific, Aristotle calls spontaneous event (*automaton*) the factually unintended happening which, if intended, would have been intended by a nonrational cause; and event of fortune (*tyche*), the factually unintended happening which, if intended, would have been intended by a rational agent. Latin translators use *casus* for *automaton, fortuna* for *tyche* (*Ph.* 2.5 197a5).

[21] This expression, which belongs to the language of daily life, conveys with precision the Aristotelian idea of a situation in which the desirable result is brought about spontaneously, automatically, without anyone having had to intend it, and to arrange things according to intention.

[22] *Ph.* 2.8. 198b34.

Now, in a series of random events, regularity may appear and, as long as we are dealing with a series, it can be said that things take care of themselves with regularity. But not all things behave so nicely. There are cases where order stubbornly refuses to emerge from disorder, no matter how long the series of trials. Many multitudes are such that no exposure to casual occurrences will ever cause in them the slightest beginning of order. If a box contains balls similar in all respects except that some are white and some are black, shaking the box in the most random fashion does not separate the black from the white. Should the white balls actually congregate on the right side and the black ones on the left, we would interpret this as a fortuitous event, a spontaneous or automatic occurrence which cannot be expected to verify any law of statistical regularity.

Confidence in the spontaneous creation of order, especially with regard to economic and intellectual affairs, is a well-known characteristic of the liberal mind. Just as the spontaneous operation of economic desires, free from any kind of direction or control, is supposed to procure the greatest production of wealth and its most equitable distribution, so the freedom to express error and truth is expected to assure the progress of truth and the defeat of error.

But let us inquire into the essential cause of statistical order. Again, experience shows that a phase of complete disorderliness may be a condition of regularity. The game is unfair when the die is loaded, for then the turning up of a particular face is designed, instead of being delivered to chance. The presence of design is evidenced by the fact that the regularities described above concerning (1) the relation between *a priori* and *a posteriori* probability and (2) the absolute and (3) the relative discrepancies are not verified. Yet, the disorderliness which is a proper condition of the statistical order is not its essential cause. Disorder is merely a transitional phase used as an instrument by principles of order. The statistical regularities will not appear unless the casting of the die is done at random. But antecedently to the random casting there exist principles of order whose features reappear in the statistical result, according to the law of essential causality which posits a resemblance between the essential cause and its effect.[23] The die is regular: this implies that it has, within close approximation, the geometrical properties of a cube and that it is homogeneous with regard to weight. If it is made of wood, the artisan must be sure that no knot causes any one part of it to be more dense than any other part. Also, the six surfaces of ivory have to be of equal weight. When these forms of order have been carefully assured, we can imagine two kinds of orderly results. If the die is thrown by an ideally perfect machine, and if the initial circumstances of the successive trials are identical, the same face will always come up, the individual event will be predictable. To liberate the other kind of regularity, namely, the statistical one, we need the instrumentality of disorder, and, rather than a perfect machine, we use, to throw the die, the method of the cup shaken absent-mindedly. The relation between the "spontaneous" of Aristotle and the spontaneous production of order such as we describe it, is quite clear. In Aristotle's analysis, which deals with an individual occurrence, factual order comes into existence casually, that is, by an accidental concourse of unrelated causes. This factual order is not

[23] *Met.* 8.8 1049b24; 12.3. 1070a4.

traceable to any essential cause, no matter how far we carry the regression.[24] For lack of an essential cause it fails to achieve the thing which is both the proper effect and the criterion of essentiality, viz., regularity. But in some series of random events regularity is present and must have a cause. Order alone can be the essential cause of order. If an effect is statistically regular, the disorder out of which it emerges cannot be initial. For instance, the ability of truth "to get itself accepted in the competition of the market" must have a cause antecedent to the set of random events made of men's opinions, inclinations, traditions and prejudices, objections and replies, occasional pieces of valid information and occasional errors.

From the preceding inquiries it results that in the distinguished case of positive knowledge the disorder of the "market" is preceded by a steady cause of order, namely, the communicability of truth, *in fact,* as well as *de jure.* Transcendent truth, on the contrary, does not defeat error spontaneously (automatically) in most cases; this disadvantage results from the many obstacles to the communication of truth in transcendent matters. Here, manifold error gets itself more certainly accepted than truth in the market of ideas.

To be sure, any particular statement by an individual scientist remains exposed to risks: it may be perverted by involuntary ignorance, by ambition, by stubbornness, by the power of uncontrolled imagination, by school prejudice, etc. In the exchange of scientific and technical ideas truth undergoes more setbacks than the admirers of science would like to believe. Yet the dominant fact is that the unrestricted right of scientists to

[24] St. Thomas, *Com. on On Interpretation,* 1.Les.14.

speak their mind generally suffices to insure the victory of knowledge over ignorance and of truth over error.

Assuming that, in some domains at least, the first premises of transcendent knowledge admit of entirely obvious formulation and give birth to rigorous demonstrations,[25] daily experience as well as the history of thought testify that the disorder of endless disagreement is the most frequent condition of mankind in all parts of the transcendent system. Let philosophers talk without any inhibition about being and becoming, appearance and reality, the ultimate causes of the things observable, the nature and destiny of man, free choice and the meaning of morality . . .; let them talk and write as much as they please about these and related topics, without any limitation or direction by state or church or academic organization: the least that can be said is that *truth is not going to take care of itself.* Even if true doctrines, or some fine approximations to the expression of truth, are actually represented in the dialogue of the philosophers (which may not be the case; indeed, they often are entirely absent), the powers at work in the processes of communication do not give truth any promise of help. These powers are such that opinions at variance with truth may well have the advantage. In these matters, it often happens that the apprehension of truth involves much greater difficulties than adherence to propositions erroneous in some way. In fact, the proliferation of philosophic theories is often determined, more or less con-

[25] Again, we are referring to those parts of the so-called transcendent system which fall within the reach of natural reason. However, when an inquiry is focussed on transcendent subjects, it is not always possible to proceed as if problems pertaining to Revelation do not exist.

sciously, by the desire to ease situations which would remain intolerably difficult if no alternative were offered to the ways of truth. Many hold that there is no such thing as definite truth in philosophy and that the worth of philosophical studies consists mostly in the stimulation of the mind and the progress of its self-awareness. Be that as it may, one thing is certain: whoever believes in philosophic truth knows that philosophy is a domain where the order of truth will not come into existence spontaneously. The factor which accounts for the spontaneous production of order in the positive sciences and techniques is conspicuously absent here. And what holds for philosophy also holds, in a broad variety of ways, for the other parts of the transcendent system.

All this makes it necessary to examine how the search for truth is related to what is fundamental in human sociability.[26] Again, many would say that truth and error, at least in regard to transcendent subjects, are the concern of the individual mind. But the principles laid down at the beginning of Chapter 1 make it relatively easy to dispose of this theory. Of all the considerations used in demonstrating the excellence of society, the first is the inability of the human individual to satisfy his needs without the help of his fellow men. We have seen that what holds for the biological needs holds no less certainly for those of a moral or intellectual nature.

---

[26] In any society the common good is primarily constituted by the felicitous accomplishment of the social acts which pertain to this society in strict appropriateness. Societies of diverse types—say, the church, the state, the labor union—may elicit social acts describable as common, generic, in character. In opposition to these, we are concerned with the social acts belonging, in specific fashion, to a definite kind of society—in the present context, the state.

Let us now ask whether the need for help by society is less real in the transcendent than in the positive part of intellectual life. As recalled, an ordinary student of mathematics today can solve problems which would have been insuperably difficult for geniuses of other ages. In the meantime, handy tools have been worked out and they are placed by society at the disposal of any student. The tools available to students of such subjects as philosophy may not be equally handy, yet some schools of philosophy are better than some others, and a characteristic of the better ones is that they offer the student, from the beginning of his arduous career, a wise selection of problems as well as successfully tested definitions, divisions and distinctions. Only those who had the rare privilege of wise discipline in the early stages of philosophic study realize that society does for the philosophy student things no less valuable than what it does for students in areas where much better conditions of communication obtain. If left to itself, without help from society, the individual intellect is not likely to find the most vitally needed truths, for such truths have little ability to get themselves "accepted in the competition of the market."

Granted that the wisdom of society should work toward conditions favorable to the order of truth in transcendent matters, the next question is whether *temporal* society has anything to do with such problems of truth and error. Many would hold that the issues described as transcendent concern the spiritual power exclusively. In order to answer this question we shall briefly inquire into the relation between transcendental truth and the most obvious duties of temporal society; then we shall recall some fundamentals pertaining to the very essence of social life.

No matter how divergent their final interpretations of civil society and its purposes, political philosophers generally start with the consideration that human life and property have to be protected by force against bad men with whom the methods of persuasion do not work. In a way, it is fitting to define the civil society, the temporal society, the state (here, these words are used synonymously), as a community possessing a power of unconditional coercion against evildoers.[27] At the time when circumstances allowed liberal thinkers to develop their philosophy without inhibition, the political ideal of liberalism was a state whose only functions were to restrain criminals and to make sure that contracts were lived up to. But at this point let us ask what common beliefs these purposes imply on the part of the citizens as well as on the part of the governing personnel. All would be easy if it were possible to assume that, with the negligible exception of a very few, the inhabitants of civilized nations agree on such subjects as the preservation of human life, the respect for property, the observance of contracts, the fundamental principles of family life, etc. If that much agreement could be taken for granted, it would seem natural to hold that the duties of the state can be fulfilled without any concern for what is going on in the souls of men. But experience shows that even in small and closely-knit groups disagreement can be sharp with regard to crime and good action. Here is a party of old friends who belong to the same section of society and whose background is much the same. Yet some call sheer murder what others consider altogether beneficial surgery; some call suicide what others praise as heroic sacrifice; some call exploitation and robbery what others understand to be the fully normal operation

[27] *Sum. Theol.*, i-ii. 95.1.

of the market, and some call violations of human rights what others interpret as the consequences of facts obviously designed by providence. Civil society cannot afford indifference to opinions on such subjects as murder, suicide, honesty in economic life, and justice and brotherhood in the relations between groups distinguished by color or language. A well organized police force does not suffice, under all circumstances, to protect innocent life. Recent events have shown that, given a certain state of opinion, the murder of a few million innocent persons may be carried out with the full cooperation of the police. The well mannered gentlemen who ran the Western world at the time of Queen Victoria were not so clear about those things. Indeed, if society wants to protect innocent life effectively, it must be concerned not only with external behavior, but also with the thoughts of men on various levels, the deepest ones not being excluded. Few would question the relevance of interest in the fiery speeches of a demagogue who calls for violent action. But what about the scholarly writings in which a philosopher, or a divine, endeavors to demonstrate the lawfulness of, say, mercy killing. Let us not fail to notice that questions pertaining to the preservation of human life are among the least obscure in the whole field of ethics. Even when obscurity is at a minimum, there is no guaranty that unanimity, or the quasi-unanimity which suffices for practical purposes, will be on the right side in all cases. If, instead of questions relative to life and property, we considered the ethics of marriage and related topics, obscurity would be much greater and opinions much more divided. People whose beliefs, in these matters, are firm and uncompromising, would concede that they are unable to explain, i.e., to vindicate rationally, the firmness of their beliefs. And, yet, who would question that the issues pertaining directly or indirectly to the ethics of marriage are relevant from the standpoint of temporal society?

By reflecting, no matter how briefly, on the nature of the acts which constitute the life of communities, we shall find ourselves in a better position to understand the interest of society, be it purely temporal, in the deep thoughts and feelings of men. Let us mention first the collective actions designed to bring about changes in external nature. A team of men pulling a boat from the bank of a river supplies a perfect example of a community in act. Of these men, none could cause the boat to move —a thing that the united team does easily. Next to these transitive actions that are collective by necessity come certain kinds of communication among men. Indeed, communications may be merely interindividual and may not involve the power of the social whole. Those that are social are distinguished from the merely interindividual ones by their being designed to cause communions among the men who communicate. A speech by a public person and the raising of the flag every morning in the schoolyards of the nation are clear examples of communion-causing communications. Thus, we are led to understand that the principal act of social life is immanent in the souls of men. It is a communion in some belief, love, or aversion. Imagine that men in solitary confinement are subjected to identical experiences and respond in identical ways. Their responses remain individual. In spite of similar feelings, these men do not make up a community. But when men, who know that they exist as a unit for the sake of common purposes, are aware of their common adherence to certain truths, of their common faithfulness to plans for a better world and of their common aversion to the evils that their community is pledged to oppose, then social life exists more certainly and more deeply than in any transitive action or communication. The common good is actually attained when a collective action upon external nature has brought about, in fact, the change for which it was designed. Again, there is actual attainment of the common good when a communication has succeeded in causing a communion. But, most of all, the common good exists in act when we all know and feel that we are one in adhering to a certain truth and in dedicating our lives to what we hold to be right and good.

Let us now bring together these two sets of considerations, those relative to the fact that temporal society cannot shirk concern with the thoughts of men, even on the deepest levels, and still discharge its more obvious duties—say, protecting innocent life, giving property a guaranty against evildoers and assuring some sort of dignity in marriage—and those relative to the *immanence* of what is most essential in common life, in other words, to the fact that the principal part of our common good is contained within our souls. As soon as these two sets of very simple considerations are taken together, the interest of society in transcendent issues—or some of them—becomes obvious. Who would believe that the temporal society, the society whose duty is to protect, with a power of unconditional coercion, life, property, honor, and dignity, should restrict its field of communion to what we have called the positive system: propositions of empiriological science and technique, the minimum of logic indispensable to organize experience, and rules of action carefully kept apart from the principles which might give them a meaning and a soul? The suggested restrictions amount to depriving the temporal community of what is deepest, most essential, and most vital in its common action. Against these restrictions we do protest whenever such an occasion as a public ceremony gives us a chance to commune in any of the "transcendent" propositions, relative to the rights of men, relative to the purposes of civil society, and relative to God, which make up the soul of our temporal common good. Promoting the order of truth in the social life of the transcendent intellect requires the operation of wisdom; it may be the most significant, as well as the loftiest, of all the duties intrusted to the wisdom of societies.

But the suggestion that the temporal society, the civil society, the state, could be, in any way and under any circumstances, trusted with the maintenance and the promotion of transcendent propositions seems to involve a lack of respect for what is most precious in truth. As we think of what temporal society would do if it undertook to serve truth in transcendent matters, our mind is promptly filled with repulsive pictures. We imagine a system of censorship run by men that power intoxicates. Brains are hammered by dead truths and by deadly errors, propaganda pervades scholarly work, rewritten syllabi leave out the really embarrassing questions, social pressure substitutes for certainty and probability, the call of the hero is silenced by decree, academic life, at all levels, is defiled by informing and related practices. Where the loftier kind of truth is supposed to be served, fraud and deceit prevail.

These pictures are not entirely the work of rebellious imagination. They originate in history and the difficulties that they bring forth are perennial. We have seen that in certain domains truth does not take care of itself. In some of these domains of truth society is necessarily interested. We are now asking whether social wisdom is in a position to give truth the advantage that cannot be expected from competition in the market or from any random events. It is easy to conceive of circumstances where both spontaneity and wisdom are powerless. The fact that chance cannot be depended upon does not necessarily imply that wisdom will succeed in doing what chance does not do. But how will the possibilities of wisdom be determined? Assuming that these possibilities are real and that the wisdom of society can effectively promote the order of truth in the transcendent life of our intellects, how will the ways and means of such an immensely difficult enterprise be determined? Plainly, it is up to prudence, to practical wisdom in the full sense of this expression, it is up to a judgment fully coincident with the complexity and mutability of the circumstances to answer these questions. Philosophy, even in its practical functions, does not deal with contingency. To say that practical philosophy rules human action from a distance is to use a well-grounded metaphor, and to insist that the distance is great between the last word of practical philosophy and the judgment that we need in order to know what we ought to do—we, a community shaped by the contingencies of a unique history and confronted with circumstances unprecedented in some way—is the least that a philosopher can say if he wants his listeners to know the truth about the limitations of philosophy. In issues such as the present one, long, complex, and difficult inquiries have yet to be started after philosophy has said its last word. It is too bad that the readers of the moral philosopher and his listeners often press him to

decide issues that admit of no philosophic treatment for
the simple reason that these issues involve contingency.

Over and above the considerations set forth in the preceding pages, I wish to make only one remark. In every
society some kinds of order and some processes retain in
larger amount the spontaneity, the autonomy, and the
mutability that are characteristic of life, whereas other
kinds of order and other processes are marked by a uniformity and a stiffness reminiscent of mechanical determinations. No one will question that in society some
things go on according to patterns that are more vital,
and other things according to patterns that are more
bureaucratic. This common remark may supply direc-
tions in a prudential search for the ways and means that
a particular society should use as it endeavors to promote
the order of truth. Briefly, the loftier a function, the
more strongly it demands to be exercised according to
the ways of life, and the less it admits of bureaucratic
management. As already said—though in tentative language—promoting the order of truth in the social life
of the transcendent intellect is the highest function of
the civil community. It is not a function which admits
of bureaucratic methods. It calls for the actualization of
what is most vital in society. From this consideration it
may follow that problems of truth often call for a sharp
distinction between the state and the civil, or temporal,
society—a distinction which we have not been using so
far. When a function is directly exercised by the state,
according to the ways which are those of any governing
apparatus, it is inevitably exposed to what is damaging in
bureaucracy. We can reasonably conclude that in most
cases the loftier problems of truth, which we have described as making up the transcendent system, should not

directly concern the state apparatus. Again, the state cannot leave these problems out of its consideration. In most cases, however, it will discharge its duty best by concerning itself indirectly with such things as the maintenance and promotion of transcendent truth.[28] Bu-

[28] As far as religious issues are concerned, the problem of freedom of thought and expression has been constantly perverted, in modern times and especially in the 19th century, by a particular state of affairs which can be described as follows. In several parts of the Christian world, it has been taken for granted—most of the time, silently—that the purpose of religion is to give men the additional energy needed to achieve moral decency. Accordingly, whenever temporal society gave religious belief and practice any kind of support, it was principally in view of preserving discipline in civilian and military life, honesty in economic and other transactions, the resignation of the poor and the benevolence of the rich, and some stability in family relations. All these are worthy achievements, indeed, but they belong to the moral order, which is by essence inferior and subordinated to the theological order. In many cases, peoples would rather tolerate dire privations than conspicuous absurdities. The irritating experience of reversed finality, the all-pervading feeling that the things of eternal and divine life were valued, principally or exclusively, for the sake of things temporal, did much to shape the contemporary notion of the secular state and to develop in various peoples an impassioned determination to keep the state secular. But imagine a country whose citizens commune in dedication to a religious faith. This country, in all likelihood, will not conform to the pattern of the "modern" secular state. Its public life is marked by features expressing the relation of moral and temporal life to the things of eternity. (It is hardly necessary to recall that these features admit of a great variety.) Dissenters may not like it, and prefer to live elsewhere. At least, things evidence consistency and the respect due to all forms of divine life, whether genuine or sincerely assumed. The formula of such a system is that the temporal common good includes, as its loftiest and most important component, a relation of subordination to things that are beyond time and beyond the realm of human achievements. Again, the problem of the dissenters may be acute, and admit of no perfectly harmonious solution. But, in spite of possible similarities in externals, there is a world of difference between such a society and one in which both dissenters

reaucracy should better deal with problems that are not so lofty and do not pertain so directly to the deep life of our souls.

---

and believers are constantly irked by the realization that things are moving backward, that the loftier is there to serve the less lofty, that the theological is treated as an instrument for the perfection of the moral, that the divine is subordinated to the human, the eternal to the temporal, and that ultimately the *truth* of religious belief is considered an issue of secondary importance.

CHAPTER 4

The Communication
of Excellence

ON PATERNAL AUTHORITY

Authority often substitutes for the reason and will of a human agent who, on account of some deficiency, cannot take care of his own affairs. This function of authority is primarily exemplified in the father-to-son relationship and it is fittingly named paternal. The deficiency which calls for government by another may be entirely normal, as in the child; it may result from an accident of nature, as in the feeble-minded; it may also result from the wrong use of one's free will, as in the criminal. The subject of paternal authority may be an individual and it may be a group. The good to be procured is not necessarily personal: it may be the common good of a society which, for such reasons as small numbers, poor equipment, immaturity or endless strife, proves unable to achieve self-government. No matter how important it may be, the paternal function of authority is never essential, for what makes it necessary is not any feature of an essence, but always the absence of some perfection. Because it substitutes for a deficient reason and will, paternal authority is provisional and pedagogical in character. It becomes abusive as soon as it ceases to aim at its own disappearance.[1] Its successful operation is best demonstrated when its subject no longer needs to be governed.

The issue of paternal authority has been discussed in other writings of ours[2] and will not be included in this treatise. The short summary just presented was merely designed to prepare for a clear distinction between authority's paternal function and its role in the communication of excellence. Indeed, excellence is communicated in relations of the father-to-son type. But under the present title what we propose to consider is a process independent of all deficiency. Once more we shall bear in mind a community free from ignorance and ill-will. In such a community there still is a problem of excellence to be communicated. Freedom from deficiency by no means implies equality in perfection. Moreover, if the members of a community were equal, it would still be desirable that those who are more proficient in one quality should help those whose proficiency has been of another kind to acquire this quality.

BEYOND THE ESSENTIAL FUNCTIONS OF AUTHORITY

The communication of excellence may follow strictly equalitarian ways. Of these, the most important are ex-

[1] It is hardly necessary to mention that by accident paternal authority may be limited in its power to promote the autonomy of its subject. For instance, in the training of the feeble-minded, a point may be reached where experienced persons agree that the poor fellow has actually achieved whatever amount of independence he will ever be capable of.

[2] See in particular, *Philosophy of Democratic Government* (Chicago: University of Chicago Press, 1951), pp. 7-19, or see the Phoenix edition of the same work (Chicago: University of Chicago Press, 1961), same pagination.

ample, love, and friendship. In the case of example, [
action is traceable to the sheer power of attractive patterns. In the case of love, the pattern of better action
receives additional potency from the desire of the lover
that the beloved should be moving at all times toward
higher achievements and more complete happiness.
When there is reciprocity in love, as friendship requires,
the person who gives also expects, though disinterest-
edly, to receive, and communication is marked both by a
more determinate character of equality[3] and by greater
efficacy. Let us now try to see whether the communication of excellence ever uses ways proper to authority.

There may be genuine government in a community
whose constitution does not embody the slightest tendency toward rule by the most excellent. Authority and
obedience are destroyed, indeed, by the determination
not to obey a law unless one has consented to it. They
are destroyed by the theory that the government is like
a cab-driver whose duty is to take me where I want to go
and by the ways of my own choice. They are also destroyed by the mystical identification of the self and the
community, which is the answer of Rousseau to the problem of freedom in social life.[4] But the absence of a distinct governing personnel does not impair in any manner or degree the essence of authority and obedience.

As far as the communication of excellence is con-

[3] *Eth.* 8.7. 1157b36. ". . . for friendship is said to be equality."
(Tr. W. D. Ross.)

[4] See Jacques Maritain, *Man and the State* (Chicago: University of Chicago Press, 1951), p. 17, or the Phoenix edition (Chicago: University of Chicago Press, 1956), same pagination. "So it
[the State] absorbs in itself the body politic from which it ema-
nates, as well as all the individual or particular wills which, according to Jean-Jacques Rousseau, have engendered the General Will
in order mystically to die and resurge in its unity."

cerned, direct management by majority vote admits of two interpretations. It is sometimes held that no selected person or group of persons can be so wise as the majority; in this interpretation, to obey the majority is to act according to the greatest wisdom. But in most cases the reasons brought forth to vindicate government without distinct personnel are relative to clarity, stability, the avoidance of intrigues, the balance of social forces, general satisfaction and peace.[5] Direct government by majority vote, insofar as it evidences indifference to rule by the better ones, suffices to show that the communication of excellence is not an essential function of authority.[6]

Another arrangement implying no tendency toward government by the most able is rotation in office, and still another is designation by chance. In the hereditary transmission of power, the disadvantages of dependence on chance are supposed to be at a minimum. Whereas the person of the ruler is determined by the hazards of birth, his training is entrusted to the wisdom of traditions and institutions. Moreover, nations have often fabricated all the myths needed to represent the men designed by birth

[5] See Pascal, *Pensées* (New York: Modern Library, 1941), 878. "Plurality is the best way, because it is visible and has the force needed to make itself obeyed; yet it is the advice of the least clever." For the more rationally clever counter-argument, cf. Dante, *De Monarchia*, 1.8.

[6] So far "essential" has been understood in contradistinction to "substitutional." But the role played by authority in the communication of excellence—as defined in the present chapter—is neither essential nor substitutional. It ranks above the substitutional and the essential. Since it takes place within a system of already attained perfections and aims at further development and greater perfection, it might be termed the "perfective" function of authority.

as excellently qualified for leadership. The extreme pop-
ularity of these myths—and not only among the primi-
tives—demonstrates that the ideal of having society ruled
by the best persons is not easily given up. But why is it
that rational choice, which is the obvious method when
the purpose is to designate the best, arouses such suspi-
cions that lot or heredity are so often preferred? Choice
involves great risks by reason of its uncertainty.[7] When
definiteness and stability are particularly valuable and
hard to obtain, chance is deemed safer than wisdom; but,
albeit at the cost of fabrications, the nations like to believe that the chances of birth do provide them with
rulers at least as able as any persons that rational choice
could designate.

Whatever the method of designation may be, the existence of a distinct governing personnel is likely to
entail a hierarchical distribution of persons. Hierarchy
results from the association of the principle of authority
with that of autonomy. By the principle of authority, any
process requiring unity of action and the subordination
of particular goods to the common good must be entrusted to a central and high agency. By the principle of
autonomy, any pursuit that a particular unit is able to
carry out satisfactorily ought to be entrusted to precisely
such a unit. How the joint operation of authority and

[7] The value of certainty in social relations and the wisdom of
using low-grade criteria when they alone can procure certainty,
are forcefully expressed in this fragment of Pascal: "How sen-
sible it is to distinguish men by externals rather than by interior
qualities! Of the two of us, which one will have precedence? Who
will yield the place to the other? The less clever? But I am as
clever as he, and we shall have to fight on this. He has four lackeys
and I have only one: this is visible, we just have to count, I must
yield, and I am silly if I question it. By that means we are in peace
and this is the greatest of goods." (*Pensées*, 319, *ed. cit.*)

autonomy brings about hierarchy is well expressed in these sentences of Thomas Jefferson: ". . . it is not by the consolidation, or concentration of powers, but by their distribution, that good government is effected. Were not this great country already divided into States, that division must be made, that each might do for itself what concerns itself directly, and what it can do so much better than a distant authority. Every State again is divided into counties, each to take care of what lies within its local bounds: each county again into townships or wards, to manage minute details; and every ward into farms, to be governed by its individual proprietor. Were we directed from Washington when to sow, and when to reap, we should soon want bread. It is by this partition of cares, descending in gradation from general to particular, that the mass of human affairs may be best managed, for the good and prosperity of all."[8] Because the township is autonomous *within* the county, and the county within the state, and the state within the federal union, these communities are distributed according to a hierarchical order. If each unit practiced government by majority vote, the hierarchy would be merely one of communities. But if each unit is governed by a distinct personnel, the hierarchical order concerns not only communities but also persons. Hierarchy disappears, or is at a minimum, in a state that has gotten rid of subordinate organizations and lords it over a sheer multitude of individuals. Such a state is clearly outlined in Rousseau and in Jacobinism. Showing that it is the most dreadful enemy of liberty is an ever-recurring concern in the work of Acton. As recalled at the beginning of this book, au-

[8] *Autobiography (The Writings of Thomas Jefferson,* Taylor and Maury, Washington, D.C., 1853), vol. I, p. 82.

thority has a bad name. The name of hierarchy is worse, if possible. Many would like to think that hierarchy is just a product of authority. But in fact there is no hierarchy unless the effects of authority combine with those of a principle whose name is not so bad, viz., autonomy.

Government by majority vote, a type of major significance for political analysis, is in fact an exceptional occurrence. Material circumstances (e.g., numerous population and large area) make it impossible in most cases. But independently of such circumstances, peoples generally prefer government by a distinct personnel. The most obvious reason for this common preference is the belief that politics is no exception to the law of proficiency through division of labor and specialization. All other things being equal, public affairs will be better run by men who have a particular inclination and a particular preparation for political leadership and who, after a while, are possessed of an experience in public affairs that other citizens cannot claim.

But divergencies are great, both among laymen and among philosophers, with regard to the kind of excellence expected of statesmen. Politics is often treated as if it were an art, and, accordingly, a thing foreign to morality; the political job could be done well by a morally bad man, just as a great painter may be a person of debased character. Many would even go as far as to hold that statesmen have got to do things that virtuous persons hate to do, so that power should better be in the hands of men not too particular about the morality of their means. This goes directly against the doctrine of the Greek philosophers who founded political science and philosophy. It has often been said that Aristotle's ethics is political and that his politics is ethical; this nicely

balanced proposition happens to express the case with
perfect accuracy. Any quality concerned with the good
use of man's abilities is ethical by essence.[9] A good painter
will do good painting if he wants to. But his art, which
may be placed at the service of man, may also be engaged
in immoral purposes. He may do poor painting because
he is lazy. He may do poor painting, in the most voluntary fashion, because he wants to irritate somebody, and,
for lack of motivation, he may do no painting at all. In
addition to the quality which is an art, a virtue is needed
to insure excellence in use.[10] Let us now see what happens
if the quality proper to the statesman is interpreted as
an art. If the statesman is, by hypothesis, an artist or a
technician, there must be, above him, a wise person in
charge of all questions relative to use. But *the statesman,*
for Aristotle, is precisely this wise person. Any description of the political leader as technician merely serves to
postpone the analysis of the main issue; a time comes
when we have to consider the qualifications required
for the *right use* of all the technical instruments which
happen to be of relevance in political life. Then and only
then we begin to study statesmanship. Thus, the excel-

---

[9] Let us sharply distinguish between "to be concerned with"
and "to procure." A practical science, say, ethics, does not procure
goodness in use, although it is concerned with it in essential
fashion. But prudence both is concerned with goodness in use and
procures it. Prudence is, and science is not, a virtue. Thus, what
distinguishes virtue is not essential concern with right use, which
can also be found in a science, but the ability to procure it.

[10] *Eth.* 6.5. 1140b21. ". . . while there is a virtue of art, there is
none of prudence." From the context, this concise sentence means:
one who is possessed of an art still needs a virtue—in order to make
a good use of his art—but one who is possessed of prudence does
not need a distinct virtue to make a good use of it, for prudence
is a virtue and procures the good use of itself. See St. Thomas,
Com. on Eth. (ed. Pirotta), 6, les. 4. 1172.

lence required for political government is not of the particular, but of the *human* description. It is the highest degree of excellence in the order of the things merely human.

True, those who speak of the state as if its problems were entirely technical may have in mind something different from what they keep saying. Often, what they really mean is that the ethics of public life is at variance with the principles which, by the consensus of decent people, ought to be observed in private affairs. The myth of an irreducible conflict between the ethics of man and the ethics of the state proceeds from various sources and is kept alive by its ability to manage a number of real difficulties. Taken with a grain of salt, it can be likened to those physical theories which, without determinately tracing facts to their real causes, are said to save the appearances. But here appearances are saved at the cost of absurdity, for it is impossible to postulate an irreducible conflict between the ethics of man and the ethics of the state without positing contradiction within the absolute.

It is by reflecting upon the social and political nature of moral virtues that we shall overcome this construct of manichaean imagination, the theory of two conflicting ethical systems, one of which expresses the necessary law of man and the other the no less necessary law of the state. Politics would never have been construed as foreign to morality, or as conflicting with *human* morality, if we had not first misconceived virtue as a purely private affair. The best way to perceive the ethical character of politics is to realize fully the political character of ethics. Indeed, whenever we achieve any understanding of man's social destiny, whenever we go beyond the cheap illusion that things social and political are merely means to the welfare of individuals, we virtually uphold the proposition that the ultimate accomplishments of prudence, of justice, of fortitude, and of temperance are not found in the individual man, but in the greater good of human communities.[11]

Let us now imagine a state governed by a distinct personnel and divided into autonomous units. According to the wish of the nations, government is in the hands of the best citizens, and the higher functions are entrusted to the better among the best.[12] With the excep-

[11] At this point two remarks are indispensable. (1) As already recalled, the *completeness* characteristic of the state raises difficulties which for all we know will never be solved quite satisfactorily. For one thing, this completeness is an ideal feature which does not admit of unqualified realization. Of many communities which describe themselves as independent states, it obviously should be said that, for such reasons as recent foundation and economic and military dependence, they really cannot be treated as states without serious reservations; in the case of great and old powers, reservations would be less serious, but they never would be inconsiderable. The experience of the contemporary world shows that no state is free from dependence in military, economic and other affairs. This incompleteness of every existent state is the great argument of the proponents of a world state [see Robert M. Hutchins, *St. Thomas and the World State,* in Aquinas Lectures (Milwaukee: Marquette University Press, 1949)]. (2) If man is considered in his *factual destiny*—and no practical science is true in a practical sense unless it includes such consideration— the ultimate character of the temporal society is subjected to a decisive qualification. The common good of the state is still ultimate indeed, but only within an order which itself is not ultimate. The moral virtues of the individual are animated by two relations, one to the temporal common good, the other to grace and supernatural virtues. But the temporal common good itself is subordinated to eternal life.

[12] It would be irrelevant to argue that no existent state ever conformed to this description: all human achievements are widely at variance with their ideal patterns, but whatever amount of good there is in mankind can be traced to the fortitude of the few who struggle in order that regulating patterns should retain some influence on the course of human events.

tion of the one, or the few, in supreme command, every citizen, insofar as he is engaged in the common action, is directed by persons who are supposed to surpass him in virtue and wisdom. To work under a leader whose qualifications are equal to his task is a happy experience, always remembered with gratitude. In such reasonable subordination, the whole character of a man attains to higher levels, silently, vitally, as a result of his fulfilling, every day and with all possible intelligence, the orders of the able superior. No doubt, the power of example is at work, and the role of love and friendship may be important. But here the communication of excellence proceeds also by ways proper to authority. What these ways are we shall understand by considering (1) the unique relation of authority to the common good, and (2) the meaning of obedience.

DOING WHAT THE COMMON GOOD DEMANDS

In the second chapter of this book, we raised the question of whether enlightened virtue suffices to procure the volition of the common good. We saw that it does not, as far as *matter* is concerned. The man of good will, who adheres steadily to the *form* of the common good, should not be asked to take one more step and, all by himself, to will *what the common good demands. This he could not do without impairing all the perfections connected with the preservation of the particular capacity.* Yet no one would hold that the relation of a person to the common good—this relation which intrinsically pertains to personal virtue—is complete and free from deficiency as soon as the right form is willed. Formalism is not any more tenable here than it would be in regard to the more personal aspects of moral life. In all cases adherence to the right form implies a tendency toward the right matter, but the *determination* of this tendency is effected in widely different ways according as the good to be brought into existence is particular or common. Once more, the life of an honest man is filled with problems of agreement between matter and form: being honest he wants to do what is right; and determining what is right, determining the thing in which rightness actually resides under the circumstances—under circumstances which always may be new and unprecedented in some relevant respect—is the job of an intellectual and moral virtue whose name is prudence. True, a man of good will may well err as to the *thing which is* right; by reason of contingency and unpredictability, he inevitably makes such errors once in a while. Such occasional failures are compatible with moral perfection; but practical wisdom and virtue comprise, by essential necessity, a *steady tendency* toward the exact determination of the thing in which rightness resides. From the moment a man comes to consider that he should not bother too much about determining the matter or content of good actions—since certainty in such determination is beyond his power—we know that he is light-minded and careless. His formalism destroys everything, his adherence to the form of the good not excluded. Because he does not care enough for the matter, he has come to miss the form.

As long as the intended achievement is personal, all takes place within the person. Only one capacity is involved. But two capacities are at work in the bringing about of the common good; individual good will procures the right form, authority determines the right matter. And thus *it is only by the operation of authority that the person enjoys the benefit of an orderly relation to the common good understood both with regard to form and with regard to matter.* No wonder that men of good will appreciate the privilege of working under a truly able leader. Thanks to his direction, the antinomy is overcome; the man of good will who wants to do the thing that the common good demands, actually knows what that thing is and does it. But the truly able leader, inasmuch as he is directly concerned, both in a formal and in a material way, with the good which is "greater and more divine than the private good," is supposed to be a man of higher excellence. Here, over and above whatever is done by example, love, and friendship, the communication of excellence follows a way proper to authority, for the greater excellence of the able leader consists in his adequate relation to the common good, and it is precisely this relation which is communicated in the act of taking his orders.

Consider this example: a society has recently undergone changes—say, morphological and technological—which render inadequate the traditional ways of distributing wealth. Even though we assume that all its members are free from deficiency, we do not expect them to be equally aware of the situation and of its requirements. In addition to the inequality of the native gifts, it is normal, indeed, that people should be unequally versed in economics, history and sociology, and unequally informed about technological and morphological changes. Since awareness of such changes is of relevance for determining several important aspects of the common good, it must be had, in the highest degree, by the men in authority. From this it does not follow that they should be specialists in economics, sociology and economic history; but they should have the kind of good judgment it takes to find the dependable experts, make them work, disengage from the complex of their technicalities the politically relevant data, place these data in a comprehensive picture of the general situation, and draw conclusions as to what action is desirable. A new display of governing wisdom will be needed for the measures of execution and their readjustment to circumstances which are still changing. Let us try to figure out what happens, as these processes are going on, to the good citizen who, though possessed of all the information that civic excellence implies, knows little about economic history and related topics.

He does not have, all by himself, the answer to the question, "What does the common good actually require?" If the question were directed to a people's assembly, or submitted to referendum, he would not feel qualified to answer it. But the Constitution has established a distinct governing personnel. Responsibility is in the hands of the most able. With the help of experts, the legislative assembly and the executive have succeeded in determining[13] what measures should be taken in order to meet the new situation. For the good citizen whom we are considering these measures may involve heavy sacrifice: as far as his action is concerned, he will abide by the laws and decrees anyway. From the beginning he has been eager to do what the common good required, in other words, he has been adhering to the form of the common good. But it was not his business to decide what

[13] It is hardly necessary to recall that this determination is by no means a purely intellectual affair: it is not an act of expertness, but an act of prudence and a judgment "by way of righteous inclination."

content this form called for and, further, he was not in a position to know. The question of content can be answered only by people more versed in public affairs. Thanks to the successful operation of wise institutions, such people are in power and the true formula of what the common good demands has been handed down to the citizen, with all the weight pertaining to the acts of civil authority. And this is how, when power is in the hands of the best, the expressions of higher knowledge, greater experience, and loftier dedication come to exist in the daily actions of all of us. Because the accident of evil men in power is conspicuous, we tend to become unaware of the human improvement which continually goes on as a result of the simple fact that the working of authority keeps our eagerness to serve the common good supplied with the needed determinations. Without these answers and the weight that they are given by authority, the best citizens would be delivered to confusion. Although such methods as direct government by majority vote, rotation in office, and designation by chance are fully legitimate and may be the best under definite circumstances, they remain primitive and hardly capable of conveying the benefit of mature civilization. We would go as far as to say that, in some contexts at least, civilization might be defined as the state of affairs in which the operations of authority steadily succeed in assuring the communication of excellence.[14]

[14] Let it be emphasized, however, that the good purposes served by, say, direct government without a distinct governing personnel, rotation in office, or designation by chance may outweigh the advantages of a communication of excellence organized according to the ways of authority even in a highly civilized society. But these would be exceptional cases.

FREEDOM FROM THE SELF

Like authority and hierarchy, obedience has a bad
name. The words of W. K. Clifford, "There is one thing
in the world more wicked than the desire to command
and that is the will to obey," express an opinion which,
without being common, has never lacked supporters
especially among intellectuals. But it is also a widespread
belief that obedience, which is obviously indispensable
in the life of communities and in the upbringing of the
youth, may work wonders in the progress of persons who
are already mature and good. Is it paradoxical to say that
the best approach to this problem is supplied by the
theory of freedom? The paradox exists for those who
identify freedom with primitiveness and fancy, not for
those who have understood that it consists in an active
and dominating indifference, in a mastery over a plurality of possible ways of action. According to the latter
theory, not all obstacles to freedom are external. Some—
and, in a way, the worst—lie within myself. Regardless of
what happens in external nature and in the actions of my
fellow men, I see that various forces existent in me restrict my freedom. Of these the most sublime are not the
least dreadful. Considering the lower first and then the
more lofty, let us mention the power of habit, sensuous
desires, lust for wealth, attachment to beloved things
and persons, and, in my relation to truth, excessive concern with the contributions of my own self. (Often, what
people have in view when they boast of their "being
faithful to their ideas" is not so much truth as some accomplishment of their own mind, whether it actually
serves truth or leads away from it.) We use an appropriate expression when we say that a man is a slave to the

habit of smoking or drinking, or that it is beyond his power to do without narcotics. The slavery of which we speak is physical when the organism is so conditioned that the sudden withholding of the habit-forming substance would be detrimental; if there is no threat of physical damage, but only a difficulty that cannot be overcome save by extreme fortitude, enslavement is moral and is not so complete; yet freedom remains badly restricted. The use of the word slave in such a context shows how commonly freedom is interpreted as mastery, or dominating indifference, so long as we have not been indoctrinated by the ideology of spontaneity and primitiveness. In some forms of anarchistic thought, the exaltation of pleasure derives a new dignity from its being associated with a greater freedom. The expressions "free love" and "free union" have a history which brilliantly illustrates the attempt made by hedonism, in modern times, to merge with the historical movement of mankind toward the greater freedom which befits societies in advanced stages of development.[15] But whoever thinks that, in the relation of man and woman, free union alone can keep him free, and holds that marriage would enslave him, has left out of the picture the most interesting possibility: a mastery over desire such that, for the sake of a law, for the sake of the good, for the sake of God, a man be free to choose, if he pleases, and without a strug-

[15] Notice that even though a people have attained the stage of development which causes an urge toward greater freedom, they may not be ready to make a good use of the freedom that they are irresistibly motivated to demand. Here lies a contrast which helps to understand paradoxes of frequent occurrence in contemporary societies. The question of whether the change was for the better or for the worse is left unanswered; hence, perplexity, bitterness, and the temptation to despair.

gle against overwhelming difficulties, the dignity and the
exclusive dedication of indissoluble marriage. These expressions, "free love," "free union," are dishonestly
loaded with the philosophy which interprets freedom as
spontaneity, and preferably as the spontaneity of animal
desires. If, on the contrary, freedom is understood to be
an uppermost kind of active indifference and mastery,
whoever finds "free love" and "free union" good enough
for him is but one who has chosen not to exercise mastery
over the lower impulses of his nature. That love is most
truly an act of freedom which is strong enough to stay
alive and remain in control when sensuous desires have
become inert or have changed their way. Referring to the
often-quoted text of Pascal on qualities and persons,[16]
let it be said that love, in order to be free, must be able
to concern itself with the hidden treasures that reason,
justice, and charity perceive in any person, regardless of
what happens to his "beauty," his "judgment," his
"memory," or any such "qualities." An old habit, or a
native disposition, are obstacles to our freedom if, when
we see that it would be *good* to act at variance with this
habit or disposition, we must confess that the power of
these internal forces is all but insuperable.

The human condition would be more easy to deal with
if the problem of freedom from our own inclinations
were restricted to the sensuous part of our self. But, let
us see what happens in the operations of scientific and
philosophical intelligence which stand at the peak of
intellectual life. A scholar has developed a theory. It is
new, he did not pattern it after the teaching of the old
authorities, he really initiated it, it is his own contribu-

---

[16] *Pensées*, frag. 323. (New York: Modern Library, 1941), p. 109.

tion and the thing because of which the history of ideas
forever will be different from what it would have been if
he, a short-lived individual, had not existed. He has
come to identify himself with his creation. Do not ask
him to give it up! It would amount to giving up the most
vital and spiritual part of himself. Do not ask Newton to
give up the theory of universal attraction. Indeed, there
is no reason why Newton should, for this best-known
theory of his has never been disproved. But every day
scientists, historians, and philosophers are faced by the
realization that truth wants them to give up theories with
which they are as closely identified as Newton with universal attraction. No sensuous desire is involved: the
conflict is between truth and this lofty part of the intellectual self which is dedicated to the understanding of
nature and of man. To be sure, it is hard for a narcotic
addict to break his old habit; but the history of human
thought testifies that abandoning a theory for the sake of
truth also takes a great deal of fortitude, and a kind of
fortitude less common than that of the soldier on the
battlefield. Whether this protective disposition is totally
involuntary, whether some sort of honesty is preserved,
whether it is within the physical power of the savant to
make himself independent of himself and to side with
truth are questions that we generally do not have to inquire into. Yet, it would be unwise to take the friendlier
answer for granted. Whatever the case may be—i.e.,
whether the obstacle to the success of truth is physical
and invincible or merely moral—freedom to welcome
truth, without hindrance on the part of our mind, certainly is a rare privilege. That human freedom should be
restricted in this high order of the mind's relation to
truth is a moral and metaphysical disaster of the first

magnitude. Knowing is the creature's best chance to overcome the law of nonbeing, the wretchedness inflicted upon it by the real diversity of "that which is" and "to be." A thing which is not God cannot *be* except at the cost of *not being what it is not*. It cannot be except by being deprived[17] of indefinitely many forms and perfections. To this situation, knowledge, according to St. Thomas' words, is a remedy, inasmuch as every knowing subject is able to have, over and above its own form, the forms of other things.[18] This remedy is, so to say, complete in the case of intellectual knowledge, for intelligent beings can have the forms of all things and *be* all things spiritually, intentionally, transsubjectively, objectively. In the order of judgment as distinct from that of mere apprehension, objectivity is one with truth, and a shortcoming in the knowledge of truth is a failure to achieve this objective and infinite existence by reason of which man is said to be an image of God. No doubt, the intellect's drive toward the infinity of truth and objective existence often is interfered with by desires pertaining to the sensuous part of our self. Of this men are aware. Failure to live by the truth because of passions is a common and well known disorder. But how much greater, how much more profound and radical the disaster when a favorite idea, a theory with which I have become identified, a system of my own, instead of leading my mind to truth acts as a screen between truth and the mind! Here,

---

[17] The idea of privation is not taken here in its fully determinate sense. (Aristotle, *Met.* 9.1. 1046a31; *Com.* of St. Thomas, les.1, 1785). The forms and perfections that a creature is denied by reason of what it is are not *due* to this creature, and it is not an evil for it not to have them. The error of Leibniz' theory of "metaphysical evil," is to see an evil in what is mere limitation.

[18] *On Truth*, 2.2.

the defeat of knowledge by subjectivity originates in the intellect itself. The most desirable of all freedoms is the freedom to be all things, as becomes a faithful image of God. No condition is dearer to the spirit than freedom from the matter-like impulses which so often force upon us the narrow capacities of subjective existence.

Is there any method, any decisive measure by which the most hidden and unnatural power of subjectivity might be defeated, so as to say, once and for all? Understanding the significance of this problem is easy, as soon as we have realized what an absurd disaster takes place whenever truth is defeated by forces of subjectivity residing in the mind itself. Let it be granted that in human affairs any achievement is precarious; what we call a good condition, in most cases, is made of endlessly repeated victories over adverse forces which keep resisting annihilation. Yet, some determinations are possessed of such profundity, and deal so directly with the root of the trouble that they can be credited with a sort of definitiveness. Thus, we are asking whether there is any way to assure the steady defeat of subjectivity in that elevated part of our being whose law is altogether one of trans-subjective existence.

Obedience may well be the closest approximation to a general method for dealing with the weight of subjectivity in the uppermost part of our self. There are many forms of obedience, and their distinguishing characteristics are relevant to the discussion of the present issue. One type of obedience corresponds to paternal authority, another to the essential functions that authority exercises in community life. The necessity of obedience may result from a membership that has not been freely chosen and it may result from the free decision to be a member of a particular community. Finally, obedience may be chosen on account of some excellence of its own.[19]

In their action toward their common good, the members of any community give and receive orders. Here, obedience consists in my steady determination to let the rule and form of my action be one with the order issued by those in charge of common affairs. My preference and private judgment will be of no weight as long as orders are what they are. Faithful obedience finds its reward in the goods of common existence and common action, but this may not be the whole story. We are now asking whether, beyond the goods of community life, obedience, by reason of its own nature, does something for the law-abiding citizen. The virtue of obedience implies that my own judgment is irrelevant in any normal[20] relation

[19] All of these types play a role in religious life. Novices, who are not necessarily young people, go through a phase of paternal government for, in the spiritual way as represented by their particular calling, they are like children and the direction that they are given bears the characteristics of paternal authority, being substitutional, provisional, and pedagogical. Of course, the essential functions of authority are exercised at all times. But every religious, besides being willing to satisfy the conditions of his apprenticeship and those of active membership in a community, is supposed to be lovingly concerned with the distinct merits of obedience, with the things that obedience can do for him over and above the goods of spiritual training and those of community life.

[20] The word normal is inserted here in order to exclude those extreme cases in which it is lawful and perhaps obligatory to act at variance with orders that are plainly absurd or criminal. We do not propose to elaborate on the problems raised by the fact that things bearing all the externals of law and therefore called "laws" may really be no laws at all for lack of justice, and that an agency bearing the externals of authority, and therefore called authority, government or administration, may be ungenuine and have no real power to command obedience.

of myself to authority. Consider, for example, the amount
of tax I shall have to pay, say, in the capacity of land-
owner. I may have ideas of my own as to the reasonable-
ness of the tax regulations. I may agree that they are perfectly reasonable, or claim that the tax is excessive, or
have no opinion. Anyway, the formula issued by public
powers is the form of my action. No disobedience is involved in my judging that the tax is excessively high.
Should it be said that obedience is concerned only with
exterior acts? Such is the position of Aquinas, who de-
clares that, as far as interior acts are concerned, no man,
but God alone, can claim the obedience of man.[21] Let it
be remarked, however, that when an exterior act is voluntary, its form is something interior to the mind and
heart of man, namely, a judgment. The rule of obedience, which covers exterior acts also covers, by strict
necessity, the judgment which is one with the exterior
act inasmuch as it constitutes its form. This is an altogether practical judgment—as practical, indeed, as action itself. On any other level than that of complete
practicality, judgment is free from any duty of obedience
to man. This means, for instance, that I may thoroughly
disagree with the principle embodied in our tax legisla-
tion; I also may agree with its principles but not with
their application to such a case as mine; I may be determined to do all I can in view of obtaining a reconsideration, by the legislator, of the system which affects me so
adversely; I may cheerfully hope that this is the last time
I have to pay such a high sum. The only thing I cannot
do is to hold that willingness to pay does not fall under
the precept of obedience.

[21] See appendix.

Thus, even though obedience is due to God alone in the domain of interior acts, there is one kind of judgment which is covered by the obedience that man owes to man. True, this judgment is not a purely interior act, since it is the form of an external action; yet its being covered by a duty of obedience implies a decisive surrender on the part of the self. All that is exacted by pirates is money or merchandise, but whenever an act is done out of obedience, I will that any judgment and volition of mine should yield, if necessary, to the judgment and volition of those in charge of the common good. The decisive step has been taken. Inasmuch as the practical judgments, which are the forms of my exterior actions, also are acts of my mind and will, the rebellious moods of my subjectivity are curbed, and this happens voluntarily and freely. Whatever excellence is communicated in the exercise of authority uses ways of distinguished significance, for the ways of obedience are kept in order by a constant process of emancipation from the powers which threaten most profoundly my freedom to do what I please for the sake of the law, for the sake of the good, and for the sake of God.

CHAPTER 5

Afterthoughts on the Bad Name of Authority

We saw, at the beginning of this book, that general objections to authority often arise from lofty sentiments. We now propose to consider what answers to these objections can be derived from the philosophical analysis of the subject.

The common good is central to every theory of authority. It is only in relation to it that authority exercises essential functions, i.e., functions whose necessity does not result from any evil or deficiency, but from the nature and the excellence of things human and social. Accordingly, if a philosophy of society dispenses with the notion of common good and is satisfied with any of the substitutes worked out by the imagination of philosophers and political scientists,[1] there will always be something awk-

---

[1] Roughly and in most cases, these substitutes are built after either of two patterns. In individualistic theories, the substitute for the common good has the character of a mere means to individual welfare. In theories opposed to individualism, whether they retain the expression common good or not, the substitute has, sometimes in a subtle and inconspicuous way, the character of a thing undistributed to men and really external to man.

The reader makes the difference between cursing the notion of

ward, to say the least, about the vindication of authority. Let it be emphasized, further, that the theory of authority as agency wholly concerned with the common good is connected with the excellence of particularity. Insofar as the particularity involved is that of the subject, not that of the function, the theory of authority comprises a vindication of autonomy on all levels. There would be nothing paradoxical about this if more attention had been given to historical relations between some forms of conservatism and some trends commonly described as "anarchistic." In their fight against the modern state, against the growing tendency to treat issues by the method of distinct functions and to let public powers assume a growing multitude of functional duties, in their fight for the preservation of independent management by strongly organized families, conservatives not infrequently displayed almost anarchistic dispositions. Occasionally they could be blamed for failure to acknowledge genuine requirements of order in circumstances which no longer were those of the old times. On the other hand, when an anarchist happens to be not a utopian but a profound thinker with an intuitive sense for social realities, his language may resemble that of a conservative. The case of P.-J. Proudhon is the most significant of all. Some socialists bitterly denounced him as a conservative in disguise, and toward the end of his short life he liked to declare that after having been the most revolutionary thinker of his time he wanted to be the

authority, which any philosopher or political scientist or journalist or adolescent can do, and escaping the vindication of authority. Unless such a vindication is present, though perhaps in veiled language, a theory of society would be too devoid of verisimilitude to meet the elementary requirements of scholarly appearance.

most conservative. To be sure, he did not contemplate any conversion, any retraction of earlier pronouncements: he felt that at a certain level of profundity and at a high degree of maturity the best of revolutionary thought and what is best in conservatism supplement one another. These final remarks of the "anarchist" philosopher should not surprise. Any appearance of contradiction with the statements of his earlier periods vanishes as soon as we think of his constant defense of family rights, of autonomous organization in all forms, and of his intensely worried struggle against the thing that democracy seemed to him bound to generate,[2] namely, the system of functional order which we have come to know as the totalitarian state. The relation between his revolutionary exaltation of autonomy and his sense for the worth of old mores and institutions, precisely considered as embodiments of autonomous life, are well suggested by these words of Georges Sorel, "All agree that the most beautiful pages of Proudhon are those in which, as he tells episodes of his existence as a working man, he discloses the bottom of his Old Frenchman's heart; his last ideas about property are entirely dominated by the recollections of the farm life that he had known in Franche-Comté. . . ."[3]

The connection between autonomy and authority

---

[2] In his discussion of democracy, Proudhon almost always bears in mind Jacobin patterns characterized by totalitarian ambitions. Rousseau, Robespierre, and Louis Blanc are the ideologists of what he means by democracy. In fact, his own political ideal is close to the democracy of independent farmers recommended by Thomas Jefferson. But Proudhon knew little about American history, and Jeffersonian democracy plays no role in his discussion.

[3] *Matériaux d'une théorie du prolétariat* (Paris, Rivière, 1921), p. 243.

would appear clearly enough if it were not that in many circumstances the word authority is taken in distinct reference to the pursuit of something else than the common good. St. Thomas contrasts dominion over free men and dominion over slaves in the following terms: dominion over free men is exercised either for the sake of the governed—as in the case of children—or for the sake of the common good; but dominion over slaves is exercised, at least principally, for the sake of the person or persons in power.[4] To call "authority" the latter kind of dominion, whether exclusively or by preference, is unwarranted, arbitrary, and altogether abusive. Whenever we speak of the "dominion of exploitation," for this is what the *dominium super servos* of St. Thomas means, let us designate it by unmistakable expressions and refer, in all our judgments, to the distinct problems of the case. Is such a dominion ever fully justified? If never fully justified, does it have to be tolerated, in many instances or in a few? Is there, in the movement of history a tendency to make it less frequently inevitable? Is there any likelihood that it ever can be ruled out entirely, save in case of sheer violence? All these are relevant questions and very important ones indeed. They all concern a particular kind of dominion, and it is not only confusing, it is absurd to lump them together with the problems of authority.

Most of all, authority is distrusted or hated by souls that have a sense for truth and feel that reliance upon witnesses, especially if these are men in power, corrupts this loftiest of all human sentiments, dedication to truth. Of course, nothing can be done for people who do not

[4] *Sum. Theol.*, 1.96. 4.

really care and are satisfied with formulas which "work," procure peace of mind, and result in a smooth adjustment to social circumstances. But considering the souls that care for truth, it should be said universally that belief in authority has the character of a substitute and a preparation for an understanding or a vision that is not yet possible.[5] Unless this substitute is treated as provisional and pedagogical, the most sacred kind of order, the order of truth, is subverted.

For the understanding of authority in matters of truth, much could be done by Christians if they realized better the relation of their faith to the promised vision. Christian faith merely substitutes, provisionally, for clear knowledge: statements of the Holy Scripture on this subject are unmistakable, "We see now through a mirror in an obscure manner, but then face to face."[6] "Now faith is the substance of things to be hoped for, the evidence of things that are not seen."[7] The center of Christian life is not found in faith and authority: it exists in a world of clear intuition. But between this true center of Christian life and our present condition there stand death and much natural dread.

[5] Even on the highest levels of scholarly life, it is often necessary to trust authorities permanently, for we are short of time and our versatility is limited. But this state of affairs, no matter how important it may be factually, has the character of a sheer accident and does not embody any principle.

In the case of the historical event, dependence on authority is permanent. But the authority involved is that of the mere witness who cannot give orders to anybody.

[6] I Cor. 13.12.

[7] Heb. 11.1

On the Meaning
of Civil Obedience

"And, thus, in what pertains to the interior movement of
the will, man is not bound to obey man, but only God.—But
man is bound to obey man with regard to things that are
effected outwardly through the body."—*Sum. Theol.*, ii-ii,
104.5.

In a paper entitled "An Ambiguity in Professor
Simon's *Philosophy of Democratic Government*" (*The
Philosophical Review*, April 1952), Professor Arthur E.
Murphy offers a very thorough discussion of the views
expressed in my book, *Philosophy of Democratic Government*, on the moral duty to obey the civil authorities.
The ambiguity that he perceives can be described as follows: against the theory that the government takes its
orders from the governed and can be likened to a cab
driver who carries his patrons where *they* want to go—a
theory which, as recalled in the present treatise, eliminates the substance of authority and obedience—I emphasized the genuineness of political authority and the
fact that the governed are bound in conscience to obey
their lawful government in the lawful exercise of its
powers. Then I inquired into the origin of the duty to

obey the political government. Of this duty God is the cause, but it remains to be decided whether power is directly conferred by God upon the governing persons or upon the community as a whole. In the first part of the alternative, the role of men in the constitution of political authority would consist merely in a designation of persons. This *designation theory* applies to the supreme spiritual authority, and some kings would have liked to believe that their own case was at least as good as that of the Pope. (See, in particular, the short treatises of Cajetan, *De comparatione auctoritatis Papae et Concilii,* and *Apologia de comparata auctoritate Papae et Concilii,* republished together, Collegio Angelico, Rome, 1935.) In the second part of the alternative, there would be *transmission,* by the community, to the governing person or persons, of a power belonging primarily to the community itself.[1]

To perceive the relevance of this analysis, let us reflect upon the familiar expressions, "divine right" and "sovereignty of the people." The upholders of the "divine right of kings" generally mean that the king receives his power from God directly, and that the people are not, in any way, the cause of his power. St. Thomas, Cajetan, Bellarmine, and Suarez oppose the theory of the divine right so understood. They hold that political power, which comes from God indeed, belongs first to the people and does not belong to any particular person or persons except by an act of transmission. But for many

[1] On the subject of the contrast between the transmission and the designation theory, I am greatly indebted to the lucid expositions of Heinrich Rommen in his important book, *The State in Catholic Thought* (St. Louis and London: B. Herder Book Co., 1945).

upholders of the "sovereignty of the people," the divine right theory is essentially constituted by the proposition that God is the cause of political power. I pointed out that if such were the case, the conscience of the governed would not be bound any more than the people in the back seat are bound to obey the leadership of a cab driver. The "sovereignty of the people" theory, so understood, would represent political government as a case of leadership without authority.

The ambiguity discussed by Professor Murphy concerns the right and power of man to bind the conscience of man. I may have used, on this subject, expressions that were not clear enough to rule out all ambiguity. Professor Murphy observes: "We are tempted, in the context, to suppose that it is the moral cogency of the claim itself which, as addressed to the consciences of the governed, elicits a distinctively ethical motive for obedience. If this were in fact his meaning, Professor Simon's argument would be a quite straightforward one, though somewhat oddly phrased. The good of a political community requires the exercise of authority and warrants the claim of its rulers to obedience in the performance of their appropriate functions. . . . To deny that political officials can rightly 'bind consciences' would be, on this interpretation, to deny that there is a moral obligation to political obedience, that the governed are ever *bound* to obey" (p. 204, *op. cit*). This is, indeed, my meaning and the way I wish my exposition to be interpreted. Professor Murphy quotes the following words from my book, "The proposition that a man can bind the conscience of another man raises a very great difficulty: far from being obvious, it is altogether devoid of verisimilitude. This is the very essence of the problem which we propose to examine; on the one hand, it seems impossible to account for social life without assuming that man can bind the conscience of his neighbor; on the other hand, it is not easy to see how a man can ever enjoy such power" (p. 204, *op. cit.*, and Simon, *op. cit.*, p. 145). Professor Murphy states the problem with the greatest clarity in the following sentences (p. 200): "The crucial instance of such ambiguity is the doctrine of the 'binding of consciences' as a power essential to the proper exercise of political authority. Does this mean that in a democracy, as in any organized political community, there is a moral obligation to political obedience—that citizens are bound in conscience to obey the commands of the agents and agencies of government in those acts that fall within the proper limits of political control? Or does it mean that the moral recognition of obligation *as binding is itself an act of obedience* [italics mine] to authority and as such properly subject to the command of those whose status confers on them the power to bind the consciences of their fellows?" The second part of the alternative is most certainly excluded, and if my expressions were not sufficiently clear, it may be because the theory that the duty of obeying political authority is itself caused by an act of political authority never came to my mind. No doubt this duty is antecedent to any command elicited by man and proceeds from a divine command. When this is clearly seen, it remains to be determined *in what ways* persons invested with political power have come to possess a power which, by divine command, and not by any act of a human authority, we are bound in conscience to obey. More precisely, the role of men in the establishment of this power of man over man has to be determined. Cajetan shows with all desirable clarity that the case of the king is not at all the same as that of the Pope.

In both cases the duty to obey originates in a divine command, but the power of the Pope is not in any sense whatsoever caused by men. It comes from God directly, immediately, and exclusively. The Pope is the Vicar of Christ and is not in any way the vicar of the Christian people; in the case of his authority, the only thing that men cause is the conjunction of a certain power with a certain person, in other words, the designation of the person who is to exercise a power. In the case of the political ruler, on the contrary, power itself is caused by the people; the king is the vicar of the people, for the first agent to be invested with political authority is not any particular person but the people as a whole. This "transmission" theory, a very old thing indeed, seems to safeguard adequately three indispensable truths: (1) political leadership is not, like that of a cab driver, one without authority; (2) it is only by act of God, *not by act of any human authority,* that man is bound in conscience to take orders from another man; (3) the first bearer of political authority is not any distinct person but the political community as a whole.

Professor Murphy seems to suggest that I consider the cab-driver theory, the one which eliminates the substance of authority and obedience, as the *liberal* theory of authority. Indeed, it has been held, in varying degrees of clarity and consistency, by many liberal thinkers. But it does not seem to belong constantly to the historical reality named liberalism. A number of thinkers universally considered typical representatives of the liberal trend would, no doubt, reject the cab-driver theory. Tocqueville and Lord Acton are good liberals; it would not occur to anyone that their theories of political authority are of the cab-driver description.